JUNK VALUES

ERIKA CLEGG

Published and Manufactured by Softwood Books

EU Responsible person: Maddy Glenn, Office 2, Wharfside House, Prentice Road, Stowmarket, Suffolk, IP14 1RD

www.softwoodbooks.com, hello@softwoodbooks.com

EU Rep: Authorised Rep Compliance Ltd., Ground Floor, 71 Lower Baggot Street, Dublin, D02 P593, Ireland

www.arccompliance.com, info@arccompliance.com

A CIP catalogue record for this book is available from the British Library

Text © Erika Clegg, 2025

All rights reserved.

Without limiting the rights under copyright reserved above, no part of this publication may be reproduced, stored, or introduced into a retrieval system, or transmitted, in any form or by any means (electronic, mechanical, photocopying, recording or otherwise) without the prior written permission of both the copyright owner and the publisher of this book. This book was created without the use of artificial intelligence tools. The author does not grant permission for this manuscript to be used for training AI models or other machine learning purposes.

Paperback ISBN: 978-1-0681509-8-2

For David Sheepshanks CBE DL,
my treasured mountain guide, who
helped me to start this ascent.

CONTENTS

PROLOGUE	1
MY STORY	11
Four stages	13
THE PROBLEM	31
A short modern history of values	33
The junk food epidemic in numbers	41
The link	49
Junk values	57
So what? *Why junk values are bad for you*	65
Horse's teeth	81
THE SOLUTION	91
Slow values	93
So what? *Why slow values are good for you*	109
Hen's teeth	125
The human onion	139
The heat and the hunger	151
Use your energy	159
CONCLUSION	171
APPENDICES	177
The top 100 most overused values words	179
Junk values field spotter's guide	183
Glossary of terms	191

PROLOGUE

PROLOGUE

'Most values statements are bland, toothless, or just plain dishonest. And far from being harmless, as some executives assume, they're often highly destructive. Empty values statements create cynical and dispirited employees, alienate customers, and undermine managerial credibility' (Patrick Lencioni, *Harvard Business Review*, 2002).

I couldn't have said it better myself. Team management expert Patrick Lencioni's statement exposes all that's wrong with most of the things that happen in the name of 'values' in company life. Made not grown, built from a surface-level process limited to a single team, worked up from a limited vocabulary of words, all launched with the inevitable outcome of creating discord, not harmony.

The growing impact of AI models is making it worse: I am seeing increasing numbers of values sets with all the telltale signs of ChatGPT having been the creative mind behind the words. This is leading to greater ubiquity amongst values. And the impact of this slapdash approach is positively dangerous.

Because without the right values, you can't even begin to build a robust and effective culture.

The situation has only intensified since Lencioni's warning in 2002. In the last two decades, increasing political fractiousness, the 2008 financial crisis, and the advent of social media (with the subsequent rapid rise in un-nuanced arguments and conspiracy theories) have decimated trust in institutions and our trust in each other.

The 2025 Edelman Trust Barometer revealed that six in ten people now carry a grievance against business, government, and the wealthy. They believe the system works for the few, not the many. And this grievance corrodes trust. With it, people view business as 81 points less ethical and 37 points less competent than those with a lower grievance level. That is the real-world cost of hollow promises and lazy values work, and people with responsibility for teams are underestimating how quickly cynicism sets in when words are not matched by action.

At the same time, Edelman found that where trust is strong, grievance melts away and optimism grows. When people can believe in the values of an organisation and see them lived consistently, they regain confidence in the future, perform better at work, and feel part of something greater than themselves. Naturally I am delighted by this research demonstrating that values are the cornerstone of trust, reputation, performance, and growth.

Done right, they are a company's most powerful asset. Done wrong, they are **junk**.

That's why when I talk about values, I am not referring to things that are purely in place to help us be better, nicer people, but things that are the necessary checkpoints to be us at our best. That may well cover kindness, but it's just as connected to excellent performance, to strong commercial outcomes, to success, and to winning. Values support excellence and it's up to you to define what excellence means to you before you think about your values. Start with the end in mind, as American business guru Stephen Covey said.

In 2017, the research firm Gartner set out to discover whether corporate culture was genuinely embedded in organisations. The results are shocking, though not, perhaps, surprising. They found that 69% of team members simply didn't know what was expected of them when it came to culture. A further 87% felt they understood it but didn't really care about it. And 90% weren't behaving in ways that reflected it, even if they thought they were.

These gaps in knowledge, mindset, and behaviour connect to build a non-culture from non-values.

Research by Qualtrics in 2022 confirms that meaningful values can even overshadow compensation. They found that 54% of North American employees would take a pay cut to work at a company with better values, and 56% wouldn't even consider a job at a company whose values are misaligned with their own. LinkedIn research a year later showed that 68% of professionals in Europe wanted to work for companies that share their values, of which nearly 90% of Gen Zers and Millennials say they'd leave a job to work somewhere that better matches their values.

And let's look at the opportunities that companies are missing. What happens when business does close those gaps? Gartner's study revealed a 9% increase in financial performance, an 8% improvement in attracting and keeping the right people, 16% rise in reputation, and a whopping 22% growth in people's performance.

The world is full of people who say, quite understandably, that values are nonsense and culture is a construct. The world is fuller still of people who, with the very best intentions, prove them right by generating values sets too quickly, without deep reflection or creative thinking, and then fail to build a successful working culture from them, as they are not effectively worked into the daily life of the organisation.

You may be one of them.

And it's not just about business values. Personal values allow us to make tough choices with integrity, to shed the dreaded imposter syndrome, to build trust and live a life we can be proud of. If you have words and phrases in mind for your own values – which you are more than welcome to keep secret – then you know, whatever the circumstances, you will act with integrity.

Yet personal values suffer the same clumsy ubiquity as corporate ones.

At a recent masterclass, my host invited the group to consider their personal values. Surely a bunch of bright, thoughtful people doing very different jobs would be shaped by different values if they really dug deep enough? But out of a table of 16, 12 offered the same word: 'integrity'.

Not one person questioned this. Around the room it seemed to strike no one as odd that exactly the same catch-all word was the obvious moral anchor for three-quarters of the room.

But can that really be true? Can twelve people's lives and decisions all be guided by the same neat label?

There is nothing at all wrong with having integrity. In fact, I would argue that anyone who lives by their values – whatever those values are – has it. Incidentally, at the time of going to press, the chef Gordon Ramsey appears to have thrown his integrity to the winds by advertising a Burger King burger after years of advocating for good food. Comments online include: 'He's a massive grifter at this point. He's money obsessed and has sold out his soul to the highest bidder.'

But that one exact same word being the go-to reference point for twelve very different people who have really thought it through is highly unlikely.

The truth is that, whether you are considering your personal or company values, you need to be willing to ask difficult questions, dwell in uncomfortable places, and challenge yourself to be better. My process for this is summed up in three brief phrases.

> Dig deep.
>
> Aim high.
>
> Be true.

This book unwraps the errors that have become embedded, without challenge, in the system and process of values. It shows you exactly what I define as Junk Values and why they cause such damage to your people, your business, your profits. And it guides you towards a better way of doing things. Because the way I advocate is neither easier nor faster but very definitely better.

Let's begin with a story. My story. As I look back on my life so far, I can see some clear phases of my own understanding and work with values, which are a helpful frame on which to build.

I never thought about values as a child or young adult, although I was brought up in a world shaped by beliefs. And once my team started to consider values in the business I owned, we used the obligatory language and put it in a website footer. But as I gained more experience in my work and my wider life, I realised that values, done right, could make all the difference. Now, they are my singular focus.

My approach has always been to explain complex topics through accessible metaphors. And the more I have worked with values – done right and done wrong – the more I have seen the correlation between them and food. The sort of chemically manufactured rubbish that's making Britain the sick man of Europe, and its antithesis: real, slow, nutritious, and flavoursome food that takes knowledge to find and patience to make.

At the end of every chapter you'll find three questions. These are designed to help you bring what you have read into your own thinking about values, culture and everything else this entails.

What does excellence mean to you? How much are you motivated to reach it?

Do you think the values you have in place at the moment are high quality and unique enough to do a great job?

How can you make your values work harder for a living?

MY STORY

Chapter 1

FOUR STAGES

On my 17th birthday, I took my first driving lesson. Three months later, I lost my way.

I hated driving lessons. Truly hated them. On my very first one, I drove into a lay-by on a motorway bridge just to draw breath, much to the surprise of my driving instructor, Jeff.

They didn't get much better. My anxiety, a constant companion from the age of seven, went into absolute overdrive. In the hours before each lesson, my stomach turned to liquid, my thoughts spiralled into worst-case scenarios, and I found it hard to breathe. Every time, I prayed that Jeff would cancel. He never did.

So, I kept going. Grimly three-point-turning, hill-starting, and emergency-stopping like my life depended on it, white knuckled from gripping the steering wheel.

Which it did. Because those driving lessons were all that stood between me and freedom.

ROOTS

Home was strict, with clear guidelines and a rhythm. Good home-cooked meals and snacks verboten. Clear guidelines to right and wrong, Them and Us, what is said and what stays hidden. Silence is golden. Anger is not allowed. But alongside these controls and confines, there was good.

Getting stuck into your community was a given. Putting other people's needs first was a defining rule. Recognising need and helping, irrespective of the circumstances, was expected. My father had an extraordinary ability to hold very strong views and yet entirely put them to one side when that was the kind, human thing to do.

We lived in an old-fashioned farming village in the Lancastrian hills. It was in many ways an idyllic, innocent upbringing that held onto the community behaviours that in other places were long lost. Village school, church on Sundays, country pub, and Beetle Drive at the Village Hall. Daisy chains in summer and conkers in autumn. Stopping to chat, whatever your age and whatever theirs. It was the kind of place where if you fell off your bike, someone would call your dad and he'd be there to comfort you before you could really start crying.

We children walked to each other's houses across fields, built dams in streams, climbed to the top of the quarry hill to watch lightning over Blackpool in the far distance, jumped off hay bales, vomited cider on cows at parties.

It was also the village where my lonely Southern mum, stranded Up North, drank to replace the friends she missed from Down South. The village to which my dad – the

Northerner – returned only occasionally from work that took him mostly to Italy, often accompanied by suave Italians, cashmere draped across their shoulders, and tales of high jinks in Perugia and Rome.

A teenage girl, increasingly trying to find her place in the world, and a miserable, gin-sodden mum were never going to be a great combination. Home with its secrets and sorrows became intolerable.

There was a bus once a day out of the village, once a day back in again. Sometimes, it just didn't come, or worse, didn't return. So, driving was the only way to escape these gloomy confines.

A couple of months into the lessons, Jeff decided I was ready for the exam. But then, horror of horrors – when my booking came through I hadn't been allocated Pass-me-Palmer, but instead, the examiner who instilled fear into the heart of driving instructors and their pupils the length and breadth of East Lancashire. His name evades me, but I'm sure it was Voldemort.

As the day loomed, all the standard symptoms arrived in triplicate. If the God I had been brought up with loved me at all, surely something would happen to get me out of it!

He did and it did. The exam was cancelled thanks to appalling weather and rebooked for another day, and in another sign of Godly power and love, the allocated examiner was the famously gentle Pass-me-Palmer, who lived up to his name.

I was free.

That's when I discovered junk food.

JUNK

The McChicken sandwich at Maccy Ds was my first weak spot, always with an apple pie chaser. BK did a chocolate milkshake that tasted like it had brandy in it. A chicken zinger from KFC became my hot choice, Wimpey's spicy bean burger its seemingly healthy counterpart. The chippy halfway between our school and the boys' school sold chip barms, and the bakery round the corner from it did an excellent vanilla slice.

On Friday nights, armed with 50p for a Coca Cola and Youth Hostel cards as dubious proof of age, we swarmed to a nightclub that sold doners with heaps of chilli sauce. On the way home, my best friend and I stopped at the Chinese takeaway for sweet and sour chicken and a spring roll so large that, even in our gluttony, we had to share.

Meanwhile at home, my growing independence was rewarded with a limitless supply of Bird's Eye boil-in-the-bag curries, Findus crispy pancakes, and low-gravity Belgian stubbies. I once drove 16 miles to get a bag of Frazzles. The delight of fast food retailer packaging, the buzz of the outlets with their clatter, chat and pop music, was matched joyfully by the hit of sugars, salts, fats, and e-numbers.

A year later, university came. Missing out on Cambridge, I hot-footed it to a college that looked like a French chateau on the outskirts of London, my only exercise a regular Chariots of Fire-esque circumnavigation of one of the quads at midnight, pissed. Since I was perpetually skint and you could cash a cheque at the pub, I pretty much moved in. Pints and pints of beer, pie and chips, crisps, and fags; so many tequila shots that on more than one occasion we ran out of lemons and had to use mango chutney.

When the pub was shut or no more cheques could be cashed, it was microwave burgers from the 7–11 at the bottom of the hill and chocolate bars from the newly installed Cadbury's machines on the Tube which would always disgorge more than you'd ordered if given a sharp tap.

Yes, that's right. I believe it's called theft.

Because I was unfettered and the shackles lay behind me. Headstrong in my newfound freedom from the structures, secrets, and sorrows of home, I found myself casually discarding the good too: the community, nutrition, faith and moral compass. If there was naughtiness to be found, you'd find me in the middle of it. No street furniture was safe. Casual vandalism was what passed for fun. Work was forgotten. Safety forgotten too: I'd scale the roof to reach the lightning conductor, beg policemen to arrest me on Trafalgar Square, condone entitled friends making fools of people. But no one made more of a fool of me than myself.

I was a Pre-Raphaelite in wafting skirts, cropped lace tops, Docs and rag-rolled curls, ploughing through pretentious books and ostentatiously weeping before Burne-Jones paintings in small Victorian galleries in towns that had seen their best during the Industrial Revolution. I was a Bet-Lynch-voiced goth, sitting miserable and out of her depth on a beer-stickied floor, tolerating music I hated and avoiding poppers. I was a galumphing Sloane, tweeded and silk scarved, peppering every utterance with 'glorious!' and 'darling!'.

I was out of place, losing identity, and adrift from myself: unanchored and devoid of pretty much anything but empty calories, alcoholic units, financial worries, and self-loathing.

CLIMB

My career called. From the hedonistic self-destruction of university, I was thrown into yet another new Erika. I joined an agency that focused on property, an agency built on fast, hard work, an agency that was growing at an extraordinary pace in contradiction of the recent recession. Lunch is for wimps, 6 am starts, 9 pm finishes; I still boast about the 96-hour shift. Clients shouted 'jump' and we Fosbury Flopped ourselves dizzy.

Home was a rat-infested basement flat next to a brothel, where one late, hot summer, the new soundtrack was the endless trudge of weeping Diana pilgrims from Gloucester Road tube to lay flowers at Kensington Palace; later, a flat in Clapham which shook to the pulse of the nuclear train and Eurostar and seemed surrounded by muggers.

Some projects appealed to my good side. I could draw on what I'd learned in my little farming village making sure people had access to affordable housing in their own communities, thanks to Nomura Bank selling off some of the Ministry of Defence housing stock they'd bought for a song. In fact, this work underpinned the kind of hyperlocal targeting in which my own agency later specialised.

But in others, I found myself swept up in the spirit of the times. London's skyline was surging upwards, its borders outwards, and property development had become both a cultural and financial phenomenon. Everyone was chasing growth, and I was learning fast – about markets, positioning, motivations. I sat in meetings where people were buyers, homes were units, and where the sheer pace of things left scant room for reflection. That was just how things were and you had to be fast to keep up.

Later, I spotted the patterns that would trouble me. The widening gulf between investor and inhabitant, the loss of character from place. But in the time, I was ambitious and eager to prove myself. So I stayed late, did the work, absorbed the lessons, and told myself that I was building my experience as well as my career.

Did I object? No. I didn't yet have the perspective, let alone the confidence, to challenge things. I was learning the ropes, it wasn't my place to question the market forces shaping the city or the ethos behind it. That's how I saw it. In truth, I was ambitious and caught up in the energy of it all.

So I climbed the ladder.

And what of the junk food? Could this manic energy be fuelled by takeaways? Of course not. The irony of the junk was that I had enjoyed it every bit as much as I'd enjoyed the excellent home-cooking that my mother largely managed to sustain even in the worst phases of her affliction. But food now became a bore, a chore.

I'd fill my fridge with a week of Covent Garden soup, a week of Conran pesto and pasta, a week of Waitrose curry. Because this was a time that seemed to lack flavour almost as much as it seemed to lack values.

Not Junk Values, not junk food; not real values, not real food – just getting on, hidden in hard work.

HOME

I was saved by a three-year-old girl, who, in a spotty red swimming costume, looked almost exactly like a strawberry.

Her story is hers to tell, not mine; but suffice to say that when the call came, I leapt to join her. Looking back, I can see the values I now express and live by reflected in that decision and in finding the resilience some of the situations we encountered demanded. But at the time, it was instinctive and the start of a slow journey back to myself: a better version of myself.

After a few years, her dad and I wanted to set up our business and despite the sensible place for our ambitions being London, we decided to do so in Southwold, a pretty seaside market town in Suffolk where my grandparents had lived and to which my parents had retired. It was partially our attempt to give her a stable environment that would extend her childhood and partially because we wanted to create a way to offer skilled employment in a place that can be very seasonal. There was a selfish reason too. We love the place, and after a few tough years it felt like the right choice for all three of us.

From the start, we set out to support our community, not just through employment but through work. Much of this was pro bono, whether that was participating on committees, advising local initiatives, or donating studio work. Over time, we set up identities and built networks for countless events, programmes, and societies, helping bring things to life so that they could find their feet, build their market, and flourish.

Steadily, the agency's presence and influence grew, and our ambition was satisfied not just by the wealth of regional work but also through international and exciting clients like Bollinger Champagne, Moroccan National Tourism Organisation, major political parties, utilities companies, charities, and the arts. Awards started to crowd the shelves and our PR cuttings folders were rich and full.

We built enough trust to mean that our clients would allow us to deliver the most leftfield recommendations, which saw us building water fairgrounds in city centres and projecting ghost ships onto breweries. At the very least, we could always advise clients - who generously opened up their entire organisations, not just their marketing teams, to us - to pursue a different route than the one they'd envisaged.

We lived a few miles outside Southwold, in a tall, brick building which had been the local stately home's laundry before the house was demolished after the Second World War. All you could see to the east and the west was fields and sky. And we plundered the culinary riches of the county.

Fresh fish from the harbour, fresh strawberries and asparagus from down the road, freshly baked bread and freshly butchered meat, neighbours' allotment glut shares, and the spoils of local market gardens became the norm pretty quickly. I noticed after about six months that my palette had changed, seeking simpler, more individually flavoursome food that tasted just as good on its own as in a recipe.

Over time, the business had its ups and downs – these things tend to come in waves, including The One Where I was pregnant at the same time as two senior people left to set up a competitive business and our biggest client dropped their spend by 90%. And our response to one of the downs was to focus on the company's values.

We already had a set of values, of course, tucked away in the footer of our website, which even I couldn't remember. I do recall that they were firmly in the Junk Values mode – respect, creativity, community, etc. I suspect I changed them for different situations and that no one else paid any attention to them whatsoever. I do know that they were superseded by a simple statement: Be Extraordinary, that took up a whole wall of our studio and focused our minds in the absence of anything more detailed.

But, as it became harder to manage the business, I knew we needed something better to work with, and the first stop for this was my personal values.

Having pondered these for some time, they alighted in a workshop I attended as a member of a peer leadership group. My purpose, meanwhile, had dropped fully formed into my head during the sermon one Mothering Sunday service in Winchester Cathedral. My guiding belief, or credo, emerged from recognising that the kind of work I loved – the work where I could unite expertise with passion – allowed me to sustain the focus required, as a sparker rather than a slogger, to push through challenges and deliver results.

> My purpose:
> To prosper and cause others to prosper.
>
> My values:
> Bring positive energy.
> Know what matters.
> Make the effort.
> Leave things better.
>
> My credo:
> Everything good should flourish.

And from that starting point, we were ready to build out to our company values: drawing in team members, chatting to clients and suppliers, seeking the insight of peers and supporters. All that information and colour and language and personality was invaluable.

The role I took from then on was as the guardian of our values, shepherding them towards becoming culture, nurturing every one of our team through the business strategy and values to personal growth. In all cases, this growth was up or out. Those for whom the mood felt off gradually clarified that thought and moved towards other plans.

I mentored and coached people face to face, helping each and every one of them to form a personal vision, consider the big things that needed addressing to help them get there, and, because you can't eat an elephant, implement actions that would chip away at the big things and resolve them. In some cases, that vision was of a career elsewhere, and that formed the basis of our work together. Some people couldn't picture a future at all and we followed a process to unearth it. One of those people had two plans: one that scared them and felt like pie in the sky, one that was a continuation of their existing path.

Over 18 months, we halved in size, leaving a core team of people that was growing in skill and ambition exponentially. Slowly and very carefully, we grew headcount back up by adding to this team's culture, never just for skills. I was starting to work myself out of my original role, and, observing the seismic improvements this process sparked, I was keen to focus on values work elsewhere too. At two years, we identified a core team for MBO, and at three years, the handover happened, keeping the buy-out process as low risk as possible for them. One of them is the team member with two versions of the plan, who's now living his pie-in-the-sky future.

Of course, it was never just about people. My role was also to get those values living everywhere – in our sales decks, conversations, and contracts; in our supplier selection and in formalising how things would work with them; in our marketing and everywhere around our studio and meeting spaces. Sometimes formally, sometimes with levity – from contracts to awards, from job descriptions to project planning, from community activities to talks – those values were irrevocably stitched in.

And it was in the informal moments that they took on the greatest meaning. I knew it was working when I overheard a conversation between two colleagues, framing a disagreement in the words of the values. For these two great friends, who always wanted to be positive with one another and both had high personal work standards, the words of the values removed any sense of personal criticism or subjectivity. That was for me the white smoke moment that revealed our new future.

Quite without realising it, I had delivered the first Active Ethos® programme in the highest-risk or the lowest-risk setting, depending on your point of view. It was my husband's and my business. Our family's future, not to mention the livelihoods of our team, rested on its success.

MEANING

So, what on *earth* does this have to do with you and your values?

The stories I share trace the phases of my life, each revealing the ways food and values entwine, shaping who we are and how we live.

First, my childhood. Roots. A world of clear moral boundaries, homemade food, and carefully rationed treats. But there were secrets and lies too. This was a time of living by beliefs, guided by other people's values, even by other people neglecting their own values.

Then came the swerve. Junk. A rejection of identity and my headlong dive into physical and psychological bingeing on junk, on adrenaline, on rebellion, on anything that gave a quick hit and filled the gaps.

Moving next into a space defined by competitive hard work, judged by time spent and money earned with no thought of moral choice. Climb. It was a time in which I diverted focus from my own values and plumped for food that did nothing more than fill a space.

And into a choice-driven existence, taking my family and myself off the path well-travelled and onto one we built as we went, fuelled by the products of the earth, the sea, the artisan. Home.

And that's what this book is all about.

Junk food is easy to grab, full of crap, meaningless, better not to have than have at all. It's globally available and utterly consistent, it's mindless and it separates people from place, nutrition, and discovery.

The same applies to Junk Values. They're plucked from a tiny lexicon, usually irrelevant, and often destined to be ignored or broken. When we state our values and live by them, we build trust. But when we declare Junk Values – words that don't matter to us, that aren't in our vernacular, that we haven't chosen or considered – we're almost certain not to live by them. And when we fail to live by our stated values, we break trust.

Slow food fuels us, nourishes us, helps us flourish. Sure, it places limitations on us – you can't eat local asparagus in November. It asks more of us – cleaning, chopping, stirring, seasoning, and serving in a way that shows our respect. But those restrictions and that effort are the necessary framework for something special, unique, and to be treasured. People respect slow food, they tend to remember flavoursome meals that stand out by their attachment to place and season, and the act of consuming slow food is one that brings pleasure, some challenge, and growth.

Slow Values work in the same way. They are carefully chosen, deeply understood, and truly ours. They fit our world, our work, our people. They might set limits – not everything is acceptable, not every choice is open to us – and they ask more of us than lazy words. We need to test them, apply them, and return to them when things get tough. But that discipline, that deliberate effort, is what makes them strong. It's what makes them real.

Slow Values shape cultures that last and build trust that underpins freedom and growth. They are precious not just because they're unique, but because they are deep, true and rewarding.

Which phase of your life and
leadership has been closest
to Junk Values: and why?

What experiences in your past have
shaped your instincts on values, and
are those instincts still serving you?

If you mapped your business's
journey in connection to food,
has it been fuelled by Junk
Values or nourishing values?

THE PROBLEM

Chapter 2

A SHORT MODERN HISTORY OF VALUES

Before we consider why and how values can go wrong, it's worth looking back at recent history to see how we came to be in this position. For over a century, people have recognised that organisations need something more human and unifying than numbers. Here's a quick tour through some of the stages and people involved in how that idea developed, right up to that Patrick Lencioni article in 2002.

Mary Parker Follett, 1910s
Long before HR or company culture were buzzwords, Follett was writing about the need for cooperation. She spoke of power not as power over but as power with: the ability to act together. She believed people needed shared purpose to thrive at work, which she called 'the law of the situation.' A century ago, she was already arguing that management without values was management without meaning.

Chester Barnard, 1930s

Writing in *The Functions of the Executive*, Barnard argued that the glue which holds people together is not simply rules or pay but a common purpose. He saw that without shared meaning, no organisation could last.

As president of New Jersey Bell Telephone, Barnard had observed that cooperation depended on what he called a moral code and that it was contingent on leaders to cultivate and protect it. Conversely, he recognised that people tended not to respond well to direction that disconnects from the values and purpose of the business. He called this the zone of indifference.

Philip Selznick, 1950s

Selznick took Barnard's concept further. He showed that businesses are more than simply functional machines but that they become institutions. And they do this by being infused with values that give people a sense of identity and belonging, as well as a task.

In *Leadership in Administration*, he argued that leadership's role is not only technical but moral. Selznick's view of the leadership role is to safeguard the character of the institution and prevent drift from its core purpose. He described how organisations come to embody shared commitments shaped by values as institutionalisation.

Peter Drucker, 1950s

Drucker – who was a fan and follower of Mary Parker Follett – is remembered as the father of modern management, and he insisted that businesses have responsibilities far beyond the balance sheet. In *The Practice of Management*, he argued that organisations exist to serve society, not just shareholders, and famously that 'culture eats strategy for breakfast.' Long before ESG, he was saying what many leaders still miss: values are not decoration, they are the difference between a business that thrives and one that fails.

He introduced the idea of management by objectives, but with the caveat that objectives must flow from purpose.

Milton Rokeach, 1970s

A psychologist rather than a business scholar, Rokeach made a distinction that remains useful today. In *The Nature of Human Values*, he separated terminal values, the end goals we strive for, like freedom or prosperity, from instrumental values, the behaviours and principles we live by to get there, like honesty or courage.

His *Rokeach Value Survey*, still used in leadership and cultural studies today, helped quantify how individuals and groups prioritise values. He also demonstrated that values could be consciously changed, which links into my thinking on The Human Onion (see Chapter 11).

Larry Senn, 1970s

Senn was one of the first people to use the phrase 'corporate culture', and his research showed that culture is a decisive factor in performance. He argued that leadership behaviour shapes culture, and culture shapes results. His work brought the idea of culture out of theory and into boardrooms. Ironically, it also laid the ground for the rush of shallow culture programmes that would follow in the 1990s.

Edgar Schein, 1980s

Schein defined organisational culture as having three layers: artefacts, espoused values, and underlying assumptions. His warning was clear: what you say your values are is rarely the same as what really drives behaviour. That gap between the espoused and the lived is where cynicism sets in (and is the reason my Active Ethos® method is essential).

Shalom Schwartz, 1980s

The social psychologist created the most widely recognised map of human values, known as the *Schwartz Value Wheel*. He identified a universal set of ten value types, each driven by a distinct motivation: self-direction, stimulation, hedonism, achievement, power, security, conformity, tradition, benevolence, and universalism. Plotted in a circle, neighbouring values are compatible, while opposites are in tension.

The wheel also clusters into four larger dimensions: openness to change, self-enhancement, conservation and self-transcendence. This is designed not just to help people understand what's important to them but also how to use it: a human version of rejecting values that are, as goes the old saying, simply 'words on a wall'.

Tom Peters and Robert Waterman, 1982

Their best-seller *In Search of Excellence* put values at the heart of business. They argued that the most successful companies had strong shared values, and they placed those values at the centre of their 7-S Framework, making values a management must-have. But popularity has its risks: it opened the door to the consultant-driven values statements that feel safe but can be junk, with all its accompanying risks.

Jim Collins and Jerry Porras, 1994

Their book *Built to Last* used examples of enduringly successful companies that held fast to a small number of authentic core values, guiding everything they did regardless of changing markets or leaders.

But the book had an unintended consequence. Companies felt compelled to publish values, whether or not they had done the hard work of fully discovering and living them. It was a classic causal fallacy: successful companies have values, having values will make us successful. So, what began as a study of deep, enduring culture sparked a wave of superficial imitations.

The mid-1990s onwards

Then came the corporate rush. Core values became the latest management trend, adopted wholesale by Western companies inspired by Japanese models of collective purpose. Unfortunately, many rushed through the exercise and spouted a list of standard words, and so today's Junk Values epidemic was born.

Patrick Lencioni, 2002

By the time Lencioni wrote in the *Harvard Business Review*, values statements had become so hollow that he described them as 'bland, toothless, or just plain dishonest'. He warned that empty values don't just fail to inspire, they actively damage trust and morale. His four categories of values – core, aspirational, permission-to-play, and accidental – remain a useful way to separate what matters. Lencioni was one of the first to tackle the Junk Values epidemic head-on.

The shame of this is that we knew better. From Barnard onwards, the lineage shows that values are powerful, but only if they are brought to life and not just written down. What began as a serious attempt to explain what makes organisations cohere has been turned into an ill-considered process.

And this is where I come in with the metaphor we'll explore in more depth in the next chapter. Because Junk Values are like junk food: they look appealing and quick to grab, but over time, they corrode the culture that feeds on them.

Which of the concepts in this chapter
challenges you most and why?

Where is the biggest gap
between your company's stated
values and the ones that actually
underpin behaviour?

What would you need to do
for your values to be relevant
a century from now?

Chapter 3

THE JUNK FOOD EPIDEMIC IN NUMBERS

It's easy to underestimate the destructive power of junk food, just as it is to underestimate the damage Junk Values can inflict. So, it's worth taking a sideways step to consider why the junk food epidemic matters and what's caused it.

Hot, salty fries, crispy on the outside and fluffy on the inside. The multi-layered hit of flavours you find in a burger stack. Creamy, sweet, and satisfying slurps of milkshake. Multi-spiced crunchy coating made thanks to a secret recipe. Caffeine and sugar carried through fizz. Rip, crunch, pow.

It's no wonder that so many of us love our fast food. And it's not our fault.

The fast food giants and Ultra Processed Food (UPF) manufacturers have lots of tricks up their sleeves to keep us coming back for more. And it all starts with our tendency to seek out salty, sugary, and 'tasty' food.

Junk food is designed to reach our bliss point by containing the ideal combination of sugar, salt, and fat to create a sense of intense pleasure in our brains. This triggers a dopamine release – the short-term pleasure hormone we also get from mindless scrolling, over-shopping, and other addictions – which activates the brain's pleasure circuits.

We might feel good, briefly. But it's doing us no good at all.

Big Food is doing what it can to increase sales and maximise profits. This type of quick-reward food is packed full of calories but with low levels of fibre, vitamins, and minerals. Its taste is heightened through the use of emulsifiers, preservatives, and flavours; these and other additives not only maximise the taste but also create appealing textures (what the industry rather grotesquely calls 'mouth feel') and enhance shelf life. These manufacturing processes don't just reduce costs and simplify distribution; they also make things hyper-palatable and override our full feelings, which means we just keep eating.

And the more you eat, the more this happens. Our bodies are designed to send us signals, including hormones like leptin, which regulates hunger, and insulin, which helps with our metabolism. UPFs seem to be disrupting these signals, so the more UPFs we eat, the more we crave them.

And when we are eating this stuff, we're being fed a host of other sensory clues. Everything about it is planned in detail to deliver the impact that Big Food is looking to make (growth – theirs, ours is just collateral damage) – the smell, the sound, the texture. This is food grown from strategy, not from soil.

And so we just keep coming back for more, just as the manufacturers planned. Because it's in their interests not just to make their product more-ish, but to make it super accessible.

Grab and go.

Drive thru.

Meal deal.

Grab bag.

It's food we can get to quickly, served right there and then, and eaten on the move.

It's not just about the loss of considered eating. Of sitting together, eating, and chatting. Of deliberate, slow consumption. Of the mindfulness of chopping and stirring. It's about direct health risk.

A 2025 report commissioned by the British government agency, the Food, Farming and Countryside Commission, revealed that 30% of the population can already be described as obese and that this figure is likely to rise to around 40% in the next decade.

An Environment, Food and Rural Affairs report delivered in 2024 shared that, if current trends continue, treatment of type 2 diabetes will cost the NHS more in 2035 than it currently spends on treating *all* cancers.

In 2024, Brazil's scientific institution, the Oswaldo Cruz Foundation, analysed the impact of UPFs on the rates of premature deaths in eight separate countries. The link between these foodstuffs and increasing rates of obesity, heart disease, and cancer underpinned a suggestion that junk food triggered almost 18,000 premature deaths in the UK in 2018–19. And at that time, our consumption of this type of food was considerably lower than it is now.

As healthy food tends to cost more per calorie than junk food, UPFs are more prevalent in lower-income households than wealthier ones, causing a further wedge between the haves and have-nots. The Environment, Food and Rural Affairs Committee report highlighted that retailers are deliberately and heavily promoting biscuits, burgers, and other cheap and highly processed foods, which offer the dopamine hit without the nutrition. To share just one example from fast food retailers, McDonald's spends between $4.5 and $5.2 billion a year on marketing and, in 2024, gleaned a healthy global operating profit of nearly $12 billion.

According to a report published in the American Journal of Preventative Medicine, UPFs form over half of the diet of British adults and almost two-thirds of that of teenagers. This makes Britain nearly the highest consumer of UPFs in the Western world, second only to America. Over the next two decades, this already fast-growing industry is likely to grow by a further 8.4%.

So what does this mean to you as a taxpayer? According to the report, the cost of food-related chronic disease is £268 billion: a combination of healthcare (£67.5 bn), social care (£14.3 bn), welfare (£10.1 bn), productivity loss (£116.4 bn), and human cost (£60 bn). Yes, that's over 22 times greater than McDonalds' annual profit.

To give this some context, Britain's total annual healthcare spend is £292 billion.

A 25% increase in obesity is only going to send the costs in one direction. And if the tax on food isn't paying for it, other taxes are.

It's not fair, is it? People are being manipulated by manufacturing techniques, marketing, pricing, and availability, and by societal acceptance, into consuming stuff that is actively bad for them. This is the ultimate in disempowerment: planting the sense of choice and yet creating the circumstances under which those apparent choices are pre-determined by people who do not have our welfare at heart.

I'm a capitalist. I was brought up a Thatcherite. This is not incongruent with the fact that I believe that we have a duty to each other, and this is a clear abdication of that duty.

So, what's it got to do with values? On so many levels, it has EVERYTHING to do with values. Yes, I am using it as a metaphor, but even as I write this chapter, I feel my anger growing. This is an unacceptable situation.

I'm also an optimist about this. Because there are signs of some green, healthy, delicious shoots.

A 2025 Mintel report valued the fast food outlets industry in Britain at just shy of £40 billion. It also noted a tendency amongst younger diners to choose healthy options, which has led to existing brands starting to offer some more nutritious choices and even the introduction of new healthy fast food brands. The report also noted a greater demand for sit-down, round-the-table group dining.

The Food, Farming and Countryside Commission consulted a citizen panel in 2025. People spoke of their concern about the system that squeezes farmers at one end and shoppers at the other, as well as their awareness of the system being stacked against them and towards Big Food. Awareness has to be the first step in the road to change.

Other countries have introduced on-pack symbols to demonstrate risk – black octagonal stop signs in South American countries, for example – are designed to further raise awareness and create a brief moment's pause before grabbing and going.

When I work with businesses to help them build culture through values, we talk of planting lots of seeds rather than one tree. In food too, it is this groundswell of small changes in behaviour that might just start to fight back against the junk food epidemic.

What other parallels do you see
between junk food and Junk Values?

Have you made conscious choices
to embrace better nutrition in
your life and for your soul?

What would you do about the junk
food epidemic if you had the chance?

Chapter 4

THE LINK

For years I have been frustrated by this casual approach to values: agreed too fast, without sufficient scope or challenge. I have struggled to fully communicate the change that's necessary to build a real values set, since the standard approach has become embedded. This is the difference between Best Practice and something very much better.

Founder of the Ford Motor Company, Henry Ford, said, 'If you keep doing the same things, you'll keep getting the same results', but if no one understands that the results are damaging, no one will stop doing the same thing. And the outcome of this is that values themselves have become devalued, commoditised, and untrustworthy.

The answer came to me one day as I listened to a podcast on the scourge of junk food. Not only is food a fantastic metaphor for values, but also I believe that the two are inextricably linked.

In a world where you can buy 1,000 chemically enhanced calories for £1.50 with the thoughtlessness and pace that entails, it's not disingenuous to suggest that a similar thoughtlessness applies to other choices. This default to ill-considered choice is represented by the laziness of how we use our down time, casually scrolling, all the way up to how we handle the existential moral dilemmas of our times.

This haste and lack of intellectual curiosity is exacerbated by the behaviour of our political leaders who can become susceptible to the influence of external voices and too short-term in focus. The aggressive pace of social media discourse, the rapid rise of judgement, evisceration, and cancellation by one ideology after another: these things all add up to normalise what would otherwise be considered unacceptable.

It takes a brave person to endeavour to challenge this – if you don't already follow Matthew Syed's writing in *The Sunday Times*, I would advocate doing so. And for us, as we go about our business, it takes a very strong core to make choices that buck the trend, to take a long-term view.

Little wonder, then, that we find ourselves in a world where trust is increasingly hard to find. Our politicians, global corporations, and the media are not necessarily speaking the truth. We know that hostile actors are manipulating news and reprogramming opinion to weaken the culture of whole countries and generations, with their own long-term vision firmly in mind. It is not just the countries we think of as cruelly led that endeavour to manipulate their citizens' choices.

Think of how nudge tactics were used to change our behaviour during COVID-19 pandemic, the way the now credible Wuhan leak theory was rapidly positioned as the mindset of tin-hatted conspiracy theorists. AI is serving up film of things that never happened, featuring people who were never there, people who were not remotely aware of the story until it hit social media and became 'fact'. Shit sticks, even fake shit.

What does this mean for you?

Firstly, you can't take trust for granted just because you've got a high-falutin' job title. A generation ago, respect and the freedom to make decisions without feeling the need to justify them or deliver them overnight would come with the job. But everything has changed.

The 2025 Edelman Trust Barometer underlines how far from guaranteed automatic deference has become. Seven people in ten think CEOs, politicians, and journalists bend the truth. And over half of 18–34-year-olds say hostile activism – anything from online argument to smashing up property – is fair game if they feel ignored. Among the over-55s, it is just a quarter.

The prevalence of 'work slop' - seemingly high quality work generated by AI which is actually full of holes, illogical and incomplete - is causing over half of team members to lose trust in their colleagues, according to an ongoing Stanford study (Sept 2025).

Titles don't carry trust anymore; you have to earn it from a folded-arms, prove-it-then audience.

Secondly, you need to doubt, too. Dig deeper into what you are told. Question what you read. Doubt what you see. Be aware of the impact of repeated untruths on your instinctive thought processes, expectations, and decisions. When faced by a consistent onslaught of propaganda, it takes a will of iron to hold your course. But if you want to live with a sense of integrity, to be your best, that's what you have to do.

Because trust is earned by consistency. Incidentally, that applies just as much to being consistently bad as being consistently good. Think of someone you find morally repugnant. Do they stick to their aims? Can you pretty much guarantee their response to a situation? Like them or not, that means you trust them to do what's expected. They have integrity, regardless of whether you agree with them.

The simple fact is that if our values are clear and we live by them, we earn trust.

Conversely, if our values are clear and we do not live by them – even once – the trust we have taken such painstaking steps to earn is broken. Anyone who has seen the disappointment in their child's eyes the first time they spot a parent's fallibility will know the sinking feeling of having broken trust.

And what does trust bring us? Why bother to build it, if we can instead enjoy the flexibility afforded by flipflopping?

Trust means freedom. If you are trusted, you will find you can do more without having to explain yourself. You can plough your own furrow. You can make bold choices. You will be more readily forgiven for your mistakes. If you are clear about your principles and live by them, you will find people drawn to your leadership who share a belief in those things that you hold dear. And that is also crucial.

Because part of the challenge we are facing in these interesting times is the abuse of power. Those hostile actors who are manipulating whole countries' and generations' cultural attitudes are doing it in pursuit of power. Interest groups are increasingly determined not just to make their point but to drown out the opposite view, to make its expression culturally abhorrent. This might seem to be a peculiar strategy, since to counter a challenge compassionately but firmly is a much stronger argument technique than aggression, but it is working through sheer force and spread.

The unintended consequences of this approach are already showing. There's a slow bubbling up of currently unfashionable ideologies through their extremes, expressed by people with the anger and ambition that makes them willing to clash fiercely. It's the determination and persistence of these campaigning groups that brings in people of a temperate disposition, who join through sheer despair that they are not seeing their views reflected in the mainstream. This whittling of discourse towards extremes of power is dangerous.

This is at the heart of my focus on values. If you make the effort to understand your values, you will have the tools in place to help you make informed decisions that you can trust. If you identify what matters to you, you will find yourself increasingly comfortable holding opinions informed by that insight, less concerned about opposition or what people think of you. If you know your values, you become your own most stringent critic and most steady champion.

And the fundamental thing is this: your values really are your values. I would never expect you, reading this book, to hold the same set of values as me.

A common misapprehension is that people with values must be united in them. In fact, when you begin to live more fully by your own, you may find others trying to use the idea of values against you. Not your values, but the junk assumption that values are uniform. More than once, I have had to deal with someone on social media who has attacked my choices on the grounds that 'as someone who works in the values space you should know better'. That says far more about their lack of insight than it does about my values.

If you try to live by values that are not deeply rooted in your helpful beliefs, world view, direction of travel, and principles then you will find them very hard and unrewarding to live with. You will feel inauthentic. You may feel unequal to the task. You may feel that they are so simplistic that you are no better for having them. The upshot of these things is that you do not behave in a way that is driven by your values and you lose the trust of those around you.

How do people know what to expect of you? You're unlikely to wear your values on a T-shirt, though I do know some people who have them as tattoos. People will guess what your values are through being around you. In the words of the Army Leadership Code, your values are inferred from observable behaviour. The way you move through life is a living expression of what you hold dear.

So, when you let yourself down, you are doubtless letting other people down too; and in doing so, unwittingly revealing either what *actually* matters to you or how little self-respect you have in dropping your principles in the face of temptation or challenge.

This is why it's so important to differentiate between Junk Values and real ones. Values which are not true to you are not just unuseful – they're positively dangerous. They will lead to what is rather poetically called 'cognitive dissonance', which means they tell our brains one thing whilst what exists around them tells our instinct something else.

Get the wrong values in place and you will consistently be hauled up in front of your metaphorical headteacher charged with letting yourself down and everyone else too. That's not good for your morale, and it's disastrous for your reputation.

The wrong values are the reason some people dismiss the very concept of values as BS. The wrong values are so easy to arrive at that they are more often in place than not. The wrong values are a thorn in my side, and this book is my way to put real values back onto the podium and knock the wrong ones off it into the mud.

Junk Values are the wrong values. In the next chapter, we'll find out what they are and what the solutions can be.

In a 'Prove it, then' world, what have you done recently that demonstrates your values beyond question?

If consistency is the foundation of trust, where are you tolerating inconsistency in how your values are lived?

What freedoms would greater trust buy you, and how will you earn it through putting your values into action?

Chapter 5

JUNK VALUES

You know those values words you keep seeing? They're the go-to words that come to mind when people are asked what their values are.

Some will undoubtedly pop into your head almost automatically. It's a Pavlovian reaction. Dog hears dinner bell, dog drools. We hear the word 'values'; we think 'integrity'.

To remind you, here are the 24 front-runners. (You'll find them as part of an extended list of 100 in Appendix A). I've categorised them for you:

> **Moral and ethical standards**
> Accountability
> Honesty
> Integrity
> Respect
> Responsibility
> Trust

Relational and social behaviours
Collaboration
Communication
Community
Diversity
Inclusion
Service
Teamwork

Performance and aspiration
Commitment
Excellence
Ownership
Quality

Sustainability and stewardship
Environment
Sustainability

Energy and drive
Courage
Leadership
Passion

Learning and thinking
Curiosity
Innovation

Look at corporate values and you will see these a lot. They are safe shared space in which unimaginative practitioners take refuge.

Unilever, Shell, Deloitte, PwC, GSK, and Accenture all cite integrity. Unilever describes itself as 'always working with integrity' and says that it conducts its operations with 'honesty, integrity and openness, and ... respect'.

Shell describes its values as 'Honesty, integrity and respect for people', which allows them to 'empower our staff ...'. Deloitte's values include 'serving with integrity' and also the phrase 'foster inclusion', which I am tipping for top spot in the next few years.

PwC's 'act with integrity', GSK's and Accenture's simple 'integrity' ... it all starts to feel a bit samey, don't you think? Can't these businesses be a bit more imaginative, do a bit better? They're none of them short of brains, money, or time. And these were drawn up before AI-created values started to infiltrate the space, compounding uniformity.

Why does this happen, and why does it matter?

It starts with the process of values development and the questions that are asked – by whom and to whom.

I caution against asking people to suggest what 'our values' are. The words in this lexicon show exactly why that can be a mistake. For some reason I can't fathom, the business of values has acquired a vocabulary from which people are scared to divert. And because there are also subtle disagreements about what values actually are – beliefs or aspirations, behaviours or decisions, inherited or selected, consistently delivered or occasionally achieved – people take refuge in the standard vocabulary of values. Incidentally, you'll find a glossary of terms in Appendix C.

And if the person asking is the boss of the person being asked, that gravitation to a limited values vocabulary will be compounded by the dynamics inherent in the relationship. Sometimes in the face of the unknown we take refuge in whatever predictability we can find.

> On a summer day in the mid-1980s, our neighbours were preparing to set off for their holiday. By coincidence, they were heading to their digs not far from the gite we were renting on the west coast of France, so both families were loading bags and belongings into their cars ready for the journey to the ferry and onwards to the Vendée.
>
> My parents, ever the Francophiles, were excited by the promise of snails, plats de fruits de mer, and sausages made from springy innards. Our Ford Cortina held little more than clothes, books, and bedding. The neighbours, meanwhile, were stacking the boot of their Austin Princess with baked beans, white sliced loaves, cereal boxes, and Fray Bentos pies.
>
> They knew exactly what breakfast, lunch, and supper would look like because certainty was their way of settling in. For us, it was the difference that gave the holiday its flavour.

International fast food brands have built their fortunes on global consistency. Wherever you are, you know what's in a Big Mac. You're safe. Forget the local cafés and restaurants, the food markets and street stalls – that it is indeed another country.

And what happens if you have the courage to move away from the cereal box to the boulangerie, from the salted fries to the street food? Oh, what joys await! Sure as hell you won't like everything you find. But when you try things, rejecting some and enjoying others, you'll start to find new things that bring colour to your life, give you a lifetime supply of great stories, and offer unexpected treats that nourish and delight you.

It's just the same with values. If you have the courage to go beyond the standard values words and embark on a journey to discover your own words and phrases, you're going to start to find something pretty fabulous. And guess what? Not everyone will like, understand, or value them as you do. That's perfect.

The truth is that clichéd values words are often chosen because people feel a little overawed by the 'what are our values' questions. They are not quite sure what the point of the question is – what will this lead to and how will it impact me? Ultimately, they can achieve a kind of consensus around these familiar words without too much of a struggle.

The problem is that if agreement is easy to reach, you probably have not gone deep enough. It's the values equivalent of a Jacob's Join, a Northern community tradition where everyone brings something to the table. Without planning, you end up with three trifles, a parkin, and no main course. The result is repetitive and full of gaps.

One of the most complex values projects I have delivered was with a hospice charity. They pushed back really hard on my initial recommendations because they were each thinking deeply about how the values would be deployed in their own situation. What we got to was unexpected, unique, and absolutely right for them.

Those 24 words from the values lexicon are really hard to push back on. They simply don't have the depth, the emotional connection, the meaning.

They're like junk food: quick to grab 'n' go, requiring no thought. Choosing them feels instinctive, and that's no accident.

Social psychologist Robert Cialdini identified a set of principles that explain why people say yes: reciprocity, consistency, social proof, authority, liking, scarcity, and unity. Junk Values rely on many of these shortcuts, which is why they spread so fast and stick so stubbornly.

And just like junk food, they have no nutritional benefit. They stand in the way of real discovery. They homogenise us.

Think about it for a second. How on earth are you going to stand out in a competitive world if you are exactly the same as your peers?

But it's more dangerous than mere bland standardisation. Junk Values are going to prove very difficult to integrate. You're unlikely to see a team fired up by them, customers attracted to them, suppliers taking them seriously as performance guidelines. That means that they are likely to be broken somewhere along the line – if not everywhere – leading to loss of trust.

Why make it so hard for yourself? Like so many things in life, upfront effort leads to long-term simplification.

Junk Values create the illusion of alignment. Slow Values are the engine of alignment.

Where are you defaulting to standard,
safe values language rather than
saying what you really mean?

When have you chosen
agreement rather than truth
in a values conversation?

What values would you name
if you weren't trying to be
understood by other people, but
to be honest with yourself?

Chapter 6

SO WHAT?
WHY JUNK VALUES ARE BAD FOR YOU.

You may well ask: does any of this really matter?

There are plenty of people who think that corporate values are such nonsense that the words used are unlikely to have any real impact. As long as they look nice behind reception, setting the tone when people come in that yours is a values-driven business, then they are doing what's expected of them.

And the similarities between different companies' values may feel like a desirable thing: creating a sense of belonging to the values club, united around your own versions of collaboration, respect, and diversity.

But this is the problem. Because it's not having values that matters: it's having *your* values. It's stating clearly and understandably what matters to your business and ensuring these values are upheld.

So, yes, it matters. It matters a lot.

Junk Values show lack of self-awareness

If you have not done the work of digging into your organisation to make sure that you really understand its stories, language, and mood then you are demonstrating a lamentable lack of curiosity and making life very much harder than it needs to be. Because whilst the company strategy is of course in your hands, your ability to communicate it is hampered if you don't understand the company vernacular, people's motivations, and points of connection or challenge.

Junk Values are obviously something that exists at a surface level; something that has not required a great deal of research and insight to develop. That's lazy, at the very least.

Junk Values ape a finished product

If you don't spend too much time reflecting on them, you may get the impression from a set of Junk Values that the organisational culture is sorted. But expressing your values is just the start, and if you're expressing the wrong values, that's not the start you want.

A set of Junk Values creates a misleading first impression; and you never get a second chance to make a first impression. These values sets are the corporate equivalent of a beige buffet lunch at a regional conference centre. Egg mayo sandwiches. Overcooked penne with lumpy, creamy sauce. Mini sausage rolls, if you're lucky. It's food nobody loves, but everybody tolerates. And just like those lunches, Junk Values leave you wondering what you've eaten, hungry for proper sustenance from another establishment, and slightly ashamed that you ate any of it at all.

Junk Values actively prevent change

Let's say you really need to change something in your business. If you build this around Junk Values, it is going to be tricky. Change requires a mindset shift from every person involved, and words that simply tick boxes won't be able to do this.

There's something in the process of developing Slow Values that brings people into the midst of things long before anything's launched. The sheer act of involvement helps them understand that there is a process of change in progress. It's the conversations, the active listening, the reflection of the process, and its expression in words that mean something across the business.

Bashing together a set of standard words in a meeting with the senior team and then telling everyone to fall into line behind them means that the process begins divided and lends no one the vocabulary to bridge the gap.

Junk Values are hard to remember

Junk Values are slippery things. Their sheer ubiquity makes them almost impossible to bring to mind. If your values sound like everyone else's, then what is there to remember? They dissolve into the background noise of corporate life. Nice enough words but lacking distinctiveness. And without distinctiveness, there is no reason to care, no story to share, nothing to pass on.

The truth is that Junk Values give people very little to hold onto. A list of words plucked from the standard values lexicon is just that – a list. With no context, no character, no real-life examples, they have nothing to hook themselves into in our memories.

If a value doesn't stick in the mind, it won't guide behaviour, it won't shape culture, and it won't last.

Junk Values will be mocked

If your values set consists entirely of Junk Values, then I am sorry to tell you that people will view them with scepticism.

I often see a bus delivering facilities management workers to their jobs, on which is proudly written: *Sustainable; Consistent; Integrity; Partner; Agility.* My response is to snort with laughter.

Grammatically, it makes no sense. The words follow no logical order. By the fourth item in this word soup, I can't remember what I've read and am deeply confused about what they are trying to tell me. I sense some repetition and contradiction amongst these five words, too. Two of them are lifted directly out of the Junk Values Top 24, the other three would undoubtedly feature in the Top 50.

In short, these words are not giving me faith. They're giving me the giggles. And I am a values fan. How would people who are even more cynical than me react?

Junk Values are perceived as insincere and shallow, which makes them easy to mock and equally easy to dismiss. If you really mean these things, can you find a better way to express it?

Junk Values are easy to break

Because Junk Values are not true, it's not so much that they are easy to break – it's more that they are impossible to live by. The usual list of words has very little connection to the lives those words relate to, and so the people they're intended to guide will be, at best, confused.

But, of course, we know that if you state your values and then break them, you also break trust.

It doesn't matter who it is that goes against these values. Even if, by some miracle, the vast majority of your workforce manages to tread the path of integrity, collaboration, and diversity, the one who fails will leave that impression on the people they're with – and that is the point at which the rot starts.

Junk Values fuel inconsistency

An interesting thing happens when I invite people to explain their values and to challenge each other's values. It turns out that every single word, out of the 100 from which I invite them to pick as a trigger to conversation, means a slightly different thing to every single person.

I've had people who describe empathy as the ability to manipulate others, people who describe honesty as the only option when they don't feel clever enough to lie. I've had people at loggerheads about hard work and splitting heirs about family. I've seen this happen thousands of times and it never fails to astound me.

The truth is that if your values set is a list of words, and in many cases, words selected because they are buzzwords that seem appropriate for the topic of values – rather than your own values – you will see this played out around you on a daily basis. That's assuming your people want to try to live by them. If they don't, these words will simply be ignored.

Either way, this kind of linguistic misalignment inevitably leads to clashes.

Junk Values create cultural confusion

I was invited to help a manufacturing business that had set out its values a couple of years earlier, but was struggling to bring them to life and form the high performance culture they wanted.

One of the words in their values set was excellence. On the surface, that looked credible enough. Who doesn't want to be excellent? But the more I spoke to people, the clearer it became that nobody actually knew what it meant.

In one department, excellence was interpreted as delivering innovation at breakneck speed, so they were launching new services before they were properly tested. In another, excellence meant cutting costs to the bone, so quality was being compromised in order to meet savings targets. And in yet another, excellence meant polishing and re-polishing reports until they were immaculate, even if it meant deadlines were missed.

The result was chaos. Teams were working against each other's definition of the same word. Customers were baffled by the inconsistency of what they experienced. Departmental leads were finding themselves locked in arguments about priorities because there was no common understanding of what excellence really demanded of them.

That's the trouble with Junk Values. They sound convincing but create confusion and mistrust. And when that happens, the culture becomes chaotic because nobody is really sure which way is forward.

Junk Values demand compliance

The 'how' of values is as relevant as the 'what'. Because it's not just the words of Junk Values that are a problem, it's the process through which they are developed.

Whilst it might be tempting to define your company values during an away day, retreat, or board meeting, ultimately, it's going to prove harder to use them. That's partly because people will feel these words have been imposed on them from on high.

You may well have a very compliant team. A team that smiles happily when told about this exciting new advance in the company's work and that is all too keen to find out how they can start to live by the values.

I've never met this team, and frankly, I doubt it exists. There will always be a hum of dissent, and before long, it will drown out the good intentions of the others. Why make it so hard on yourself?

Junk Values mislead new recruits

Let's imagine for a moment that a new member of the team has been drawn to your business by your Junk Values. They are struck by the particular combination of words you put up in a word cloud behind the reception desk.

Might they find the realities of life in the business a little surprising?

The probability is that your Junk Values are promising one thing and delivering another for all the reasons we have discussed. What you see as diversity might well be what they see as embedded prejudice. Your compassion may barely hit the baseline of their expectations.

This is very thin ice, by the way. At the time of writing, we are around 18 months away from a major shift in employment rights in the UK, which will mean unfair dismissal claims can be brought from the very first day of employment.

That misunderstanding could turn out to be very expensive.

Junk Values are tiring

If your values don't matter, people will inevitably disengage.

At first, they try to understand. Then, they become uncomfortably aware that they are not doing what others seem to expect. They may realise that those other people don't understand the expectations either. In time, they lose belief not only in this part of the company story but in others too. It saps their trust, their motivation, and their will to give their best.

Tired people will not perform to the best of their abilities, may become disruptive, and will most probably start to look elsewhere for work – taking a very dim impression of your business away with them.

Junk Values get the wrong people on the bus

In his iconic book Good to Great, Jim Collins uses the metaphor of a bus to explain how important it is to have the right people in an organisation. He says that great companies don't start with a strategy and then hire people to fit it. Instead, they start by 'getting the right people on the bus', which means making sure the team has the right mix of talent and character, and then putting them in the right seats, which means the roles that play to their strengths.

I'd take his metaphor further. Imagine your bus itself is giving out the wrong signals. If its sides are plastered with posters for a pleasure park, and the destination board reads SEASIDE, then of course you'll attract people who want a fun fair or a day by the sea. When they get on the bus and discover that in fact you're heading to a tough mountain climb, they'll feel misled. It's not their fault. They simply responded to what your bus promised.

In business terms, if the way you present your organisation through your brand, your values, and your promises suggests one kind of journey, but in reality you're taking people somewhere very different, you won't just get the wrong people. You'll also create disillusionment and disappointment.

Think hard about the signals you are sending out to people who are considering getting on your bus. It is much better that they never get on, than that they do and have to be asked to get off later. For them, for you, for the other passengers ... think about that signage.

Junk Values make decisions hard

Junk Values are not robust enough to rise to the occasion when you have a tough choice to make. This is ironic because one of the principal roles of values is to give you a sounding board for decisions. And they are most useful when you are caught between the devil and the deep blue sea – in other words, when neither choice is tempting.

There's an excellent business I know that nearly went belly-up in the 2009 recession. By introducing values and training everyone in the business to understand management accounts, they mounted a staggering revival with a committed team. Things were great for years and a culture of fun prevailed.

So, I was saddened when I bumped into their CEO recently. He was frustrated that the values weren't helping as the company faced new challenges in the wake of the COVID-19 pandemic. He felt that the words were wrong.

Now, in their case, they are not using Junk Values. They have phrased their values in a way that lands very naturally. But despite having had 12, and having increased this to 13 a year or so in, it still felt like something was missing.

I warn my clients about the dangers of accidental camel adoption. A camel is, according to the old saying, a horse designed by committee. It's tempting to add to your list of values when gaps seem to emerge. But the truth is that addition only creates more confusion. How much easier is it to order off a brief daily specials menu than an eight-page à la carte menu? If this business had managed to confine its values set to a lower number, the task in hand would have been easier now.

So, whether your issue is unimaginative, hastily grabbed Junk Values, or an overabundance of words, you'll find yourself without guidance when you're in a tight spot.

Junk Values make things far, far worse

This is the number one reason why people who think values are bullshit have come to that conclusion, and in most cases, I completely agree with them.

There's a famous true tale that is worth repeating, and it's about aircraft manufacturer Boeing's values and culture. Boeing's values are right out of the Junk Values lexicon. Safety & Quality. Trust. People focus. Ownership. Innovation. The warning signs are all there: grammatical inconsistency, illogical order, and the same old words. How many of the top 24 can you spot?

And how does Boeing live its values?

> **Safety & Quality:** Boeing has faced repeated concerns about safety flaws in its aircraft, including the 737 MAX's software, which was not fully explained to pilots or regulators. In one high-profile incident, missing bolts led to a door plug detaching mid-flight. The company has also struggled with quality audits and internal warnings that were not adequately addressed.
>
> **Trust:** After two fatal crashes, investigations found that Boeing misrepresented aspects of the 737 MAX programme to regulators, the public, and its shareholders.

The US Securities and Exchange Commission concluded that Boeing and its then CEO made false statements about the aircraft's safety.

People focus: Reports from multiple whistleblowers highlighted safety issues and described a culture in which speaking up was discouraged, with some alleging retaliation. High-profile cases included whistleblowers who faced significant personal and professional challenges, which sent a strong warning to others about the risks of raising concerns.

Ownership: Critics have pointed to failures of leadership and oversight. The board was seen as slow to respond and audit systems did not sufficiently flag risks. Production deadlines often took precedence over operational diligence. Even after the crashes, Boeing's focus appeared to be more on financial recovery than cultural reform.

Innovation: Analysts argue that Boeing prioritised short-term financial strategies over longer-term engineering investment. Instead of developing new aircraft, existing designs were stretched, while cost-cutting and staff reductions eroded the company's once-renowned engineering quality.

It doesn't make for cheery reading, does it?

Not only has Boeing done all these things wrong, but they can add hypocrisy to the list.

Junk Values damage your reputation
And whilst we are in this dark place, let's look at reputation.

Reputation and trust are bound tightly together. And the truth is that if people cannot trust you to keep your word, your reputation will suffer.

Strong reputations are a survive-and-thrive essential. A good reputation improves relationships, enhances marketing effectiveness, increases consumer trust and willingness to pay a premium, and helps businesses perform better and recover more easily during crises. Organisations with positive reputations attract investment, talent, and customer loyalty. But reputation is difficult to measure, slow to rebuild after damage, and increasingly vulnerable to developments like AI and political instability.

Proactive, values-led reputation management is essential. Because if you say one thing and do another, it's going to wipe your reputation out in one step.

Junk Values give ALL values a bad name

As you'd imagine this is the one that makes my teeth itch. Focusing on real, Slow Values in a world full of Junk Values is like setting up a regional foodie bistro on the top floor of an out-of-town shopping centre, in amongst the Dunkin' Donuts and McDonalds and Slush Puppy stalls. (This book is my process of upping sticks from the shopping centre and building my own venue somewhere far nicer.)

If I had a chip every time someone looked me in the eye and told me how they had done their values, usually at an off-site, perhaps facilitated by someone from their external HR contractor; how they'd all come up with their preferred values words, chosen the most repeated, and shared them with the rest of the staff; how they've got an awards scheme and a high-fiving app and mugs – I'd be fat and full of chips.

Real values carry a lot of weight, and they suffer unnecessary opprobrium because of the ubiquity of Junk Values.

When calling for Congress to overcome its challenges in 2017, Senator John McCain, known for refusing early release during his five years as a prisoner of war, said: 'Our shared values define us more than our differences. And acknowledging those shared values can see us through our challenges today if we have the wisdom to trust in them again'.

Ask yourself this: do you have the wisdom to trust in your values? Do you have values in which you can place your trust?

Could Junk Values be undermining decisions, recruitment or culture in your business? Where and how?

Would your values withstand critical feedback, or are they already creating scepticism and disengagement?

How much time, money or trust are you wasting each year because your values lack clarity and memorability?

Chapter 7:

HORSE'S TEETH

Let's say you've been offered a horse. This horse is a gift. You happen to have a stable, a field, and a lonely donkey, so you accept it gladly. And because it's a gift, tradition dictates that you don't look it in the mouth.

Why not?

Because that's how you tell a horse's age. The length, curve, and condition of its teeth reveal how many years it's lived, and inspecting a gift horse's mouth is seen as rudeness. It implies that you're hunting for flaws instead of saying thank you.

And just as you can age a horse by its teeth, you can age Junk Values by the words they use. The language gives them away.

The simple fact that they are using zeitgeisty language is a clear sign that Junk Values are the wrong values and that they'll feel weirdly outdated before too long. I could just as effectively have called this chapter 'Bathroom suite colours' or 'Hairdos' since you can instantly gauge the era in which a bathroom was fitted from its colour and find the hairstyles laughable in family photos from years ago.

Like dated fonts, clichéd straplines, and 1950s advertising, if your values are forged from what concerns the world at the time you draw them up, they'll show their age soon and their unsuitability for the task in hand sooner.

Choose buzzwords, and you're creating values that will very quickly render themselves laughably obsolete.

Why are organisations choosing these words? In my view, it's about safety in numbers. Whilst the world changes around us, as older people in business become increasingly mystified by the generations coming up behind them, when niche interest groups often define the direction of societal opinion using a word that is growing in prominence, representing these new things might feel like a necessary step.

Perhaps, they think, if we don't say we are all about 'diversity', people will think we are against it. If we didn't pick 'sustainability' in 2014, the Greens will think we're in favour of burning the earth. We may not quite know what it means, but if we say it now, we'll be able to backfill the meaning later, somehow. And at least, we'll look like we care.

I remember meeting an old acquaintance at lunch a year or so ago. An affable person, ex-military and quite traditional. He was in a new job working for a hospitality brand, one which had firmly revamped itself in the wake of the killing of George Floyd in 2020. It was now advertising anti-racism in its venues and had revamped its website to focus on diversity of opportunity illustrated with photographs of its largely Anglo-Saxon team – but no matter, intention is everything. This old acquaintance looked at me with the zeal of a recent convert and assured me that he was, and always had been, 'passionate about diversity and inclusion!'.

That was it. Those two exact words. The words in which this topic are generically couched.

So, what do I think? Let's be clear – I wholly believe it's possible for people to realise things are important that they hadn't considered before. I have moved on from opinions I was brought up not to question, by questioning them thoroughly and finding them wanting. It was not his newly acquired passion that concerned me, but his vocabulary.

Because out of deep enquiry comes true insight, and the likelihood of that taking exactly the same format as the two most used words of an era or movement? Very slim.

Whether intuitively or objectively, this feeling of discord is one we all get when the stated values do not match our experience, and it's compounded when they are couched in clichéd words. Take HSBC. In 2022, it ran a high-profile advertising campaign positioning itself as a champion of sustainability. But at the same time, it was financing large fossil fuel projects. The Advertising Standards Authority banned the ad for being misleading. That's the risk of values-as-virtue-signalling: if they're not true, you will get found out.

Of course these words are usually chosen with good intent. They're often based on a desire to please; symbolising a wish to move with the times, correct past errors, be open to change. But if you try too hard to move towards what's fashionable rather than what you hold dear, might you look a little like a dinosaur driving an electric car? In other words, rather surprising and deeply unconvincing.

The use of these popular buzzwords can reveal the approach to be empty posturing, a decision made without the depth of thinking that you'd need to understand something.

> When Chinese steelmaker Jingye bought British Steel in 2020, it promised to invest £1.2 billion and secure the future of the Scunthorpe plant. However, much of that investment never arrived, and the site continued to haemorrhage money thanks to rising energy costs and falling global steel prices.
>
> As the British government tried to push them towards using greener electric furnaces, Jingye refused a £500 million support package to help manage the transition. Suspicion deepened when the company cancelled vital raw material orders, putting Britain's last blast furnaces in jeopardy. Faced with the collapse of the UK's only capacity to produce virgin steel, which is essential for defence and infrastructure, the government passed emergency legislation to take control.
>
> It was at that point that the media was invited into the plant, and reports were full of comments about the quantity of seemingly meaningless values statements prolifically applied to walls and boards. 'Cherish our employees', 'Serve our customers' and other standard statements were written in English and Chinese around the plant: empty, ironic statements given what had just happened there.

We build our own culture. We do not follow everyone else's. Junk Values are a statement to the world that you are sucking up to the zeitgeist. And if you evidently don't trust your own judgement, who will?

DO DIFFERENT

There are other things you might be sucking up to of course. Maybe you admire Apple. (It was *always* Apple.) Maybe you think you'd like a bit of that Apple magic. So maybe you will start with 'simplicity' and 'innovation', like they did.

The problem is that this is not you, it's Apple.

By all means have other businesses' values in mind to guide your process. Like starting to redecorate your house with a few Pinterest moodboards, inspiration is great for stimulating thought, for giving you a sense of direction. It's a place from which to progress with a better idea of your own context, your assets and attitudes, experiences, and emotional points of connection.

There is a similar risk in working with a consultants' framework that lists values words to pick from. These should only ever be the starting point: ingredients for the recipe, not the final meal.

When I am giving masterclasses, we run a little personal values exercise called 'The Values Challenge'. I invite participants to pick a word from a list of 100, define it in their own words, share a story that shows how it's relevant to them, and defend or change it. The words are designed to spark thought at pace. It's a powerful exercise that is simply designed to give a taste of values thinking. It's definitely not the way to approach a serious values development programme.

Even without that list we know that if you ask people what their values are or what they think a business's values are, they are most likely to grasp words you'd find on a list.

These are the standard values words this book is designed to uncover for the Junk they are.

As a rule of thumb, if your values session results in a word cloud, you're not looking at values. You are looking at one tool out of a whole bunch of tools that help you find the way to your values.

You may pick your words so as not to offend. It's understandable, in these opinionated times, to want to choose the path of least resistance. However, if you choose vague or popular words as safe options, not only will nobody feel moved by them, but they could cause your reputational downfall. Not so safe now, right? What this approach leads to is internal apathy and external cynicism. Frankly, you are better off without stating them.

Usually, I first meet businesses when they are unsure why their values don't seem to be helping them build the kind of resilient culture they need. Of course, this will partially come down to lack of activity to make it happen. Even the best values set will make no impact unless things are planned around them to seed them into business. But it very often also comes down to the words themselves.

Think about it. You simply can't live what you don't understand. Take a word like 'belonging'. What does it mean?

Without a clear definition, it's just a word, a seed scattered on concrete. It carries the potential to grow, but it can't take root or flourish unless the ground has been properly prepared.

And it's not just a risk because you will struggle to bring it wholeheartedly into behaviours and expectations across the business. It's a risk because if you say something and fail to honour it, you'll lose people's trust. Values are promises. If you say 'authenticity' and put even one foot out of line, it's going to be all over Glassdoor like a rash.

At the very least, negative Glassdoor comments might put people off the idea of applying for a job with you before anyone wastes their time. Worse, maybe, is if the truth had not crept out into the outside world and people approach you on the basis of these values.

Let's say someone really shines in their interview and nobody on either side of the table spots the disparity between your stated values and real life. The new starter arrives and begins work. How long does it take before the scales fall from their eyes? That's when the risk begins. Some will voice their frustration and become consciously disruptive. Others will simply withdraw by showing up but doing the bare minimum, what's come to be called 'quiet quitting'. With the change in employment rights from 2027, that's a risk for the business from the day they arrive.

I do not believe that there are many bad people in this world. But values incompatibility can make lovely people feel like the very worst kind. Their disenchantment will then disrupt everyone else within the company, not to mention clients, suppliers, and other people you work with externally.

What if, by some miracle, you do manage to bend your Junk Values to fit, and they start to form your culture? The signs might look good, but what happens when things get tough? Junk Values are brittle and likely to snap under pressure. Slow Values are at their best in times of crisis: they can bend, adapt and hold. They'll underpin decisions you can trust.

> Here's how to spot Junk Values, using the **Junk Values Spotter's Field Guide**. You'll find an opportunity to do this for yourself in Appendix B.
>
> **Word watch:** Are your values full of this year's buzzwords? Could they be in a LinkedIn influencer's biography? Or are they full of buzzwords from the year in which they were developed? Find business articles and corporate blog posts from the time and see what you find out.
>
> **Blandness test:** Could any other organisation say the same thing, in any industry, and it still make sense? Could anyone actively disagree with them? Because if no one can disagree, no one will care much either.
>
> **Definability check:** Ask five people who represent different levels in your company what each value means. Do the answers line up? Are they meaningful? Do they come from those people's own experiences and insights, or do they feel generic?
>
> **Truth test:** Be honest. Were these values aspirational or actual when you chose them? Are they lived now? Could you make a tough choice using them?
>
> **Cultural consistency:** Do your hiring and firing, praising

and promoting reflect these values? Or do you have a different culture beneath the surface, which is created by other forces, forces that have stronger gravity than yours?

Story audit: Can you tell a few real stories where each value has been applied across your business, in different settings, by different people? Could these stories become part of your lore?

Reaction check: Say your values aloud in a team meeting. Do people nod or wince? Do you feel like a bit of a wally saying them?

Whilst it might be rude to check a gift horse's teeth, it's necessary to give values a good inspection. If they're too easy to date, use that as your sign to go deeper, aim higher, and be truer.

To help you fine-tune your understanding of the differences between Junk Values and Slow Values, you'll find the Junk Values Spotter's Guide in Appendix B, ready for you to fill in as you go about your business.

I guarantee that once you start to notice Junk Values, you'll see them everywhere.

Which of your values are
actually zeitgeisty buzzwords,
and how could you rewrite
them in your own language?

Would a competitor read your
values and recognise their own
in them, or would they actively
disagree because yours are distinct?

If you asked five different people
to define your values, would
they give the same explanation
or five different stories?

THE SOLUTION

Chapter 8:

SLOW VALUES

Having established that Junk Values are ubiquitous and cause more harm than good – the 1970s, normalised, not-wearing-a-seatbelt version of company culture – we can now turn our attention to the alternative.

Slow Values.

Slow Values are the considered, deeply rooted approach to values: they are grown carefully out of real experience, not plucked from a list of standard words during an away day. They require honesty, reflection, and the courage to name what really matters. Once uncovered, they nourish every part of an organisation.

Like slow food, they have provenance and are sustaining, giving people something real to work with and returning trust, loyalty, and performance in abundance. Slow Values last because they belong; they are lived daily, not launched and forgotten.

Slow Values take a long time to get to. That goes against the grain in our increasingly hasty times. Politics is short term, built round the election cycle. Careers are not for life anymore, never mind the companies that build them. Attention spans are short.

So, choosing to build Slow Values is a brave, counter-cultural thing.

To uncover these real values – Slow Values – you have to pause, look around, ask questions, and be willing to ride with the discomfort that some answers might bring. My approach is to ask for stories, not for values. Here are some of the questions that help to launch good conversations, though our goal is always to move off script as soon as possible and towards flowing easy chat that reveals some unexpected truths.

> What are we like at our best?
>
> Think of a time that happened.
> - What took place?
> - Who was involved?
> - How did you feel?
> - What happened as a result?
>
> How would you describe us?

And you're asking this not just of yourself, or the board, or the SLT, or the marketing team, or even your whole team — you're also asking this of clients and customers, suppliers and consultants, collaborators and investors, community and charities. You're looking for the whole picture, not just the internal view.

I am by no means the only person to advise stepping away from words like values when you are working on this in the real world. Many businesses have done the same, choosing terms that feel more deeply considered and connect more directly with their teams.

Recent research shows that a third of Fortune 100 companies in the USA now actively avoid the standard words like culture, opting instead for more distinctive expressions – credo, manifesto, or other bespoke phrases.

> Pepsi has Pep+.
>
> Amazon talks about its Leadership Principles.
>
> Google has Ten Things We Know to be True.
>
> My own agency, Spring, was the first to use Active Ethos®. At the time, it was a brand asset; now, it is a process.

You also need to consider context. Your values do not exist in a vacuum. Firstly, they have to survive contact with the real world, and secondly, they need something around them to justify the effort they require.

The first of those things – surviving contact with the real world – is supported by my Circles of Context models. Each of these models ties into an in-depth process of conversations and research that focuses on the circle's segments one by one, slowly building an understanding of what that segment brings to, and gains from, your values.

In the programmes I run, I provide values development participants in companies with their own workbooks that set out the sections in order, starting with 'You' and finishing up with 'Black swans'. This means that everyone involved in the process understands the necessity of this level of insight, the facts about the business, and how it fits in with their role. We use it first to analyse their opportunities and challenges, next to build their response in a contextually established way.

Hub: In your control, you and the decisions you take

You: What makes you tick, and what do you want to come out of this process?

Nuts & bolts: The incontestable facts about your organisation

Strategy: Your business strategy, broken down

Second circle: Connected to your control, people within and without your organisation

People: Your people within the organisation

Customers, suppliers, community: People external to the organisation who work and deal with you

Peers, competitors: Other organisations in the sector or with audience share

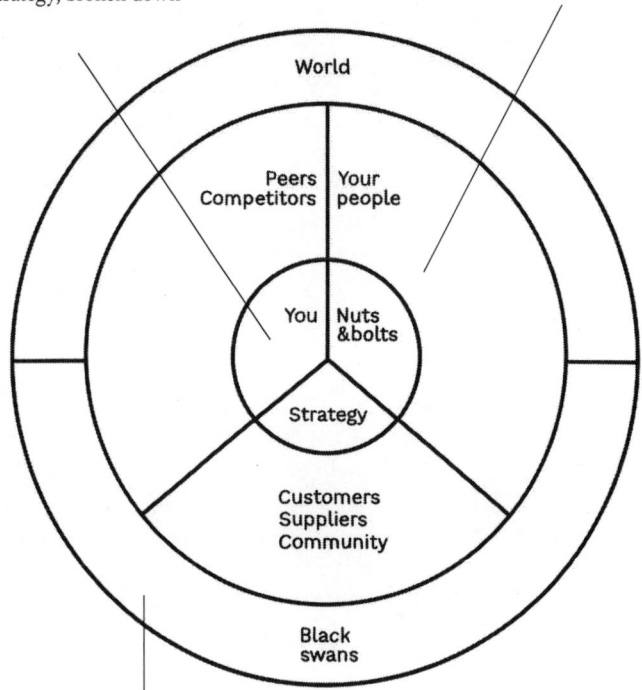

Outer circle: Out of your control and makes an impact on your organisation

World: What is happening in the world at large that will impact you

Black swans: Unexpected and potentially cataclysmic events that force change

By taking the time to work in each area of the circle, you are helping to make sure that your values are robust enough to underpin changing circumstances, people's varied levels of influence, and a broad range of motivations. Sometimes, our values can do no more than help us make a decision that maintains our integrity in the face of insurmountable challenge.

As we spend time in each of the Circles of Context segments, we ask similar questions to those listed above. We start with you, and you need to be brave enough to go deep.

Why are you doing this? Why now? Are you willing to do the hard yards it will take to get this running and keep it going? What are your hopes for the process?

My rules when I work with people and businesses are that we allow no elephants in the room or ostriches with their heads in the sand. If you are conscious that you are uncomfortable with your own answers or with those of others, that those people whose answers have given you pause are in a space that needs further investigation – then keep going.

McKinsey has a technique called the Five Whys. So do toddlers. It means not being willing to take the first answer, instead to keep pushing through until you're closer to the root of the matter. This you need to deploy as you start to investigate what it is that makes you tick, what makes the business what it is.

What are you looking for?

What you are *not* looking for is something that diverges

entirely from your vision. This is *not* an abdication of leadership. You know what you need to achieve, you know a lot – though not all – about what's working, and what's not working too. As you build up knowledge and insight through this process, you are gaining a deeper understanding of the motivations and concerns of the people you talk to, hearing their language, gauging their characters, and reading between the lines to understand the unspoken.

Having had the courage to dig deep into your own views and hopes, you tackle every other segment of the circle in turn. What are the hard facts of your business, what is your strategy?

Looking out to the second circle, what views do those who influence and are influenced by your business bring to it – what are their stories told to you or evident in their communications, and what is said about them?

And finally the circle over which we have no control, but which can have a great impact on us – the world, and those often catastrophic things that emerge from nowhere and cause us to pivot, the black swans.

I strongly recommend not doing this yourself, if you are the very head of the business. Everyone will say what they think you want them to say. Instead, bring in someone who has the ability to grasp your ambition and business needs, strong listening skills, and knows how to make sense out of and disseminate a huge amount of information.

They will need to immerse themselves in your company's strategy, communications, history, and ambitions, not to mention your competitors' narratives and what's said about them in places and platforms that they don't control like Glassdoor and Trustpilot.

All of this stuff goes into the pot. I call it filling the snow globe. If you're not overwhelmed, you're not trying. Gradually, over the course of the process, patterns start to form, sense emerges and your unique values begin to take shape.

This will help you express the company vision in a way that sparks ambition and bring your purpose to life so it builds a strong sense of meaning.

> Sometimes, you may find your purpose needs to change. Given that purpose is at the heart of our business that is an extraordinary thing to say; but it's true. Think of Kodak, think of Blockbuster. What happened to them when they didn't address their purpose?
>
> I worked with a sizable business whose multinational ownership situation meant they needed to address their purpose or run the risk of losing some of their exceptionally talented team and becoming less attractive to new hires.
>
> We flipped their purpose to become about people's growth rather than company growth. The way it was phrased set out the company's dedication to nurturing and launching the world's greatest sector talent, and they called this their 'passion' rather than purpose.
>
> My client knew that this new perspective needed support to grow, and so they launched a scholarship scheme giving people throughout the business the opportunity

> to fuel bespoke career development plans with generous training provision. Some have started bachelor's degrees, others coaching qualifications.
>
> The more they grow, the more the company benefits: and those who use this to launch themselves into other opportunities elsewhere have brought value whilst still in post and take the company's reputation forward when they leave.
>
> It's a win-win that needed a purpose pivot.

And as with any journey that leads somewhere extraordinary, you'll meet a few surprises along the way. With a clear road and the wind behind you, uncovering and defining the values – and the vision, purpose, and story that sit with them – takes about three months.

That's a quarter of a year, not just one senior leadership team meeting.

Once we know what really matters, we need to test whether the current culture embraces it or rejects it. If it rejects it, that needs work. At the time of writing, I am in the eighth month with a client who had to take a diversion to focus on succession. They've been brave enough to face their own ostriches and elephants, and, because of that, the process will serve them well.

But what of the craft? Because this is a matter of craft.

All this information you have taken the time to dig up is feeding you with a rich diet of nutrients that will help you flourish and grow. It's essential to honour that by expressing them as well as you possibly can. Think how the words you choose will live in the context you have investigated.

> How will the words, phrases, content, and order be not just unique but essential?
>
> Will those words trip naturally from people's tongues as they speak to one another?
>
> Will they earn a 'Hell, yes!' from the right people and a 'No way!' from the wrong ones?

Great values attract and repel, like magnets. They're in the vernacular of our business, not industry jargon. They are real, the opposite of bullshit. The opposite of junk.

PERSONAL VALUES

And what if you are considering your personal values? So many of the same considerations and processes apply. When I work with people we take a minimum of ten weeks – an hour a week, with homework – and more if we trip over a rock on the path.

I'd advise you to work through this with someone else, someone who feels comfortable supporting your journeying into uncomfortable spaces. Look into what really matters to you, what makes you happy or angry, challenged or bored, fulfilled or frustrated. What do other people think of you, do you think? What experiences have unlocked good things or bad things for you?

Only very late in the process do we start to look at lists of values words, and then only to underpin a conversation about how these might inform phrases that have deep meaning to us.

And what will these values phrases do for us? Whether we are talking about personal or corporate values, they have a big job. Amongst their many responsibilities, you'll find guiding your decisions, building your integrity, creating consistency, enhancing relationships, underpinning growth, providing motivation, and securing trust. They give people clarity about power dynamics and suitable choices, about expectations and outcomes.

Hub: In your control, you and the decisions you take

You: What makes you tick, and what do you want to come out of this process?

Your facts: The incontestable facts about your life

Your plans: The route you want to take, broken down

Second circle: Connected to your control, people you spend time with

Personal relationships: Your family and close friends

Professional relationships: Your colleagues, and professional advisors

Community relationships: Your neighbourhood, groups and memberships

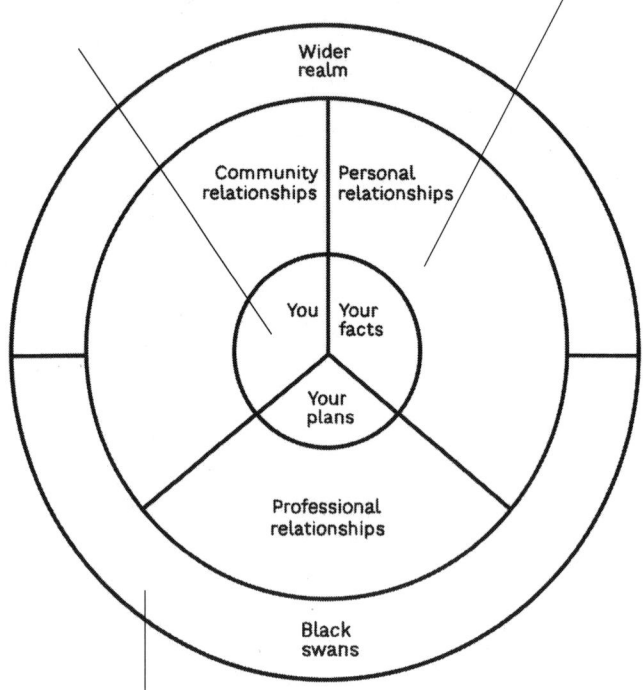

Outer circle: Out of your control and makes an impact on your life

Wider realm: What is happening in the world at large that will impact you

Black swans: Unexpected and potentially cataclysmic events that force change

Slow food not only brings us joy, colour, and flavour but also helps to make us healthy and resilient. The same is true of Slow Values.

> Of course, between junk food and slow food, between Junk Values and Slow Values, there are midpoints.
>
> You might find the values equivalent to a cook-it-yourself kit, for which a manufacturer has selected the ingredients and created the recipe for you to prepare. Better than junk, for certain, but lacking the depth of authenticity that is created by regional, seasonal, even self-grown ingredients forming a dish you can cook that's an adaptation of the recipe passed down by your granny.
>
> This kind of midpoint approach often comes in the form of a considered and well-explained description of how some of the standard single words are relevant to your business. It's better than nothing, but could be so much more you, so much richer, create so much more impact. In other words, it's a pale imitation of Slow Values.

One area of personal values that comes up often is the difference between values and beliefs. We'll discuss this in a later chapter because it's of great importance. To put it simply, beliefs are things we have gained as a result of other people's values – maybe family, possibly at school, even in our early career.

Sometimes, these beliefs are great and worth turning into conscious values. But often they limit us. Note how I mentioned Granny's recipe had been adapted?

That's essential. If you hold strong beliefs, take the time to dig in and test whether they truly fit your life's purpose.

My grandmother's stew was wonderful, but my version works better for me. It still carries the best of what she created with the resources she had, yet it also allows me to add my own preferences and ingredients. The result is a dish that feels comfortingly familiar but has become unmistakably mine.

Earlier in this chapter, I introduced two vital elements that must sit alongside values. First, they need to survive contact with the real world, which we have already discussed. Second, they must be supported by something that makes the effort of living by them worthwhile.

This second piece is at the heart of my Active Ethos® model. Active Ethos® is the relentless application of the right values, motivated by vision and purpose, to build culture. The right values – the things that I call Slow Values – only take hold when they are paired with the right motivations: an inspiring vision and a clear, essential purpose.

These are also supported by narrative.

What story can you build to contextualise this work? Stories speak to the heart whilst facts speak to the mind: stories are memorable and shareable. Organisations need stories for people to care about and retell, stories that help them to live by their values. Without a great story, your vision, purpose, and values will struggle to find their place in people's working lives.

Do your values feel like a buffet of beige food or are they a distinctive, memorable and challenging meal?

If you stopped using standard vocabulary, what words would your people or customers naturally use about you?

Do you have the courage to move beyond the usual values words and choose values that attract and repel?

Chapter 9:

SO WHAT?
WHY SLOW VALUES ARE GOOD FOR YOU.

We understand that Junk Values are bad for us but so far I haven't done much to shout about good quality, real ones.

Believe me when I say that our values – personal and corporate – are one of the most powerful weapons in our armoury against indecision, inauthenticity, failure, and guilt. They are the difference between uncertainty and clarity, between chaos and control, between reputational risk and owning perception.

Just as junk food and slow food are very far removed from one another in provenance, method, and impact, it turns out that Junk Values and Slow Values have little in common. Junk Values are bland and give short-term satisfaction with a pay-off of long-term damage; Slow Values are full of flavour and nourish all who come into contact with them.

1. Slow Values are truthful

Slow Values reflect your organisation's true character. Because they are formed carefully over a period of months, built from thorough research and insight, they demonstrate a deep understanding of what makes you, you. They are not simply a reflection of your sector or an accompaniment to what your competitors say. They have bite. They sound like you and they mean something.

This deep understanding of the principles and purpose of your business leads naturally to shared stories, told both within the company by its people and outside by its customers, suppliers, and other observers. The discipline you have shown in ensuring values are based on true insight strips away anything superfluous and reveals the heart of the thing.

This truth supports clear communications and builds your reputation. Because you have fine-tuned your words, you become easy to understand and that makes you an attractive proposition. You are you, not a copy of someone else.

2. Slow Values grow with, not on

Because they're developed with your people, not imposed upon them, your Slow Values feel part of the culture even before their expression has been finalised. Your people consider them relevant since they emerge from what those same people have shared with you. They are recognisable, feel true, and already embedded to some degree.

My clients always look slightly surprised and relieved when I tell them that we won't be launching their values in the traditional way. There will not at any point be the need for the Chair to announce 'our values' to an all-hands get-together under a banner like 'Vision 20:40'.

What we actually launch is the process of planning actions around those values to start seeding them across the business. And because they have sprung from within the business itself, this feels like a natural, authentic process, never a management consultancy initiative.

3. Slow Values sharpen focus

Partially thanks to the development process and partially because of the precision of their phrasing, Slow Values help to fine-tune your perspective.

They act as a triangulation point, helping leaders understand what's going well, what needs attention, and how to keep things progressing in the right direction. They give you a shared and accessible language to describe the culture you are aiming for, as well as a reference point to bring you back on course if things start to stray.

Because Slow Values are expressed well, they are memorable and meaningful, enabling you to make confident decisions. This is especially important when you are facing a difficult choice in ambiguous circumstances.

They also help you to spot the difference between isolated issues and signs of a deeper cultural malaise.

4. Slow Values grow from insight

You do not create Slow Values by starting with a blank piece of paper in front of you. They are the outcome of a considered process of research, questioning, listening, joining dots, and spotting gaps.

What this means is that they are rooted in what makes your business work and built on specific and regular real-world events shared in people's stories, rather than created using theories or via brainstorms.

Values formed this way are simply an expression of the kind of behaviours that earn trust, underpin performance, and build reputation within your business. Because they are grounded in evidence, they're believable and usable.

> When Pia Sinha found herself helicoptered into 'Britain's worst jail' as Governor in 2017 – HMP Liverpool, which was also described as 'squalid' by Peter Clarke, then the Chief Inspector of Prisons – one of her first actions was to get values in place to guide the steps that needed to be taken.
>
> To this day, it's one of the best values sets I know.
> - Rebuilding Trust.
> - Creating Hope.
> - Believing in the Future.
>
> There are just three of them and they use clear, simple words. And not only do they express what needed to be done to get the prison back on its feet again (which she did, with the full involvement of her team, prisoners, and the community), but it also goes to the heart of what the prison service needs to do for people who have made bad choices and ended up there.

They turned the perception of prison from an end into the first step on a better path.

5. Slow Values are bespoke

You can spot Junk Values because you will most probably see at least one of the 24 standard values words. These are the words that people reach for when asked to express values, un-nerved by the question and keen to please.

In the FTSE 350, the top five values words you'll see are collaboration, integrity, respect, innovation, and excellence. Around 50% of FTSE 350 firms have collaboration as a value. These words feature time and time again, irrespective of sector or brand.

You can spot Slow Values because they are the antithesis of this single-word uniformity. Slow Values have not only required effort to ensure that their content is correct but also to adapt their phrasing to reflect the vernacular of the business.

They will not include clichés or buzzwords from the top 24 values words. They are an evocation of the company's own lingua franca. That's because Slow Values are designed to be understood and spoken aloud by everyone from frontline staff to the boardroom, and that requires them to be moulded to fit, not for your people to change the way they communicate.

6. Slow Values are magnetic

Magnets attract. Magnets also repel. Just as sales is the art of getting to 'no' quickly (thanks to American sales guru and motivational speaker Zig Ziglar) so are values. Because the less time and money you spend on customers, suppliers, and team members who are not going to help you grow in the right direction the better, as it frees you up to focus on those who will.

> BrewDog, the beer business, found itself in hot water a few years ago when a group of disgruntled staff and alumni revealed some of the less savoury aspects of working life at the brewery. It's fair to say that BrewDog's leadership made things worse with its initial responses, too. All in all, the business did not cover itself in glory.
>
> But the truth is none of this needed to happen if BrewDog had stuck to its first four 'unofficial' values – of which two are 'We bleed craft beer' and 'We blow shit up' – because, frankly, any member of staff who wanted to complain about a tough working environment could have been gently led to the sign on the wall behind reception and asked to think again.
>
> 1. We bleed craft beer.
>
> 2. We are uncompromising.
>
> 3. We blow shit up.
>
> 4. We are Geeks.
>
> 5. Without us, we are nothing.
>
> They didn't. That fifth value smacks of afterthought. 'Without us, we are nothing'. A noble sentiment. And an open door to complaints about the employee experience.

There are plenty of people in the world who want to join new, rising start-ups. They want to experience the energy, be part of the growth story, take on the challenge, get it on their CV. I did it myself in my mid 20s, when I joined a fast-growth branding agency whose owners' reputation went before them. If you are clear about it, you will not inadvertently attract people who are not up for that type of employer. Simple!

7. Slow Values already exist.
Slow Values often formalise what's already felt but not said. They express the rhythms, instincts, and gut feelings that shape how a company really works when it's at its best. Unlike sudden leadership announcements or SLT away days wading through post it notes, Slow Values emerge over time through considered questioning and expert listening.

When you ask people outright what the company values are, they'll usually take refuge in buzzwords from the Junk Values list. These words don't capture the grit, humour, drive, or care that actually fuels the place. So, instead, you listen differently, at different times and with a different set of people. You collect stories, paying attention to the language people use about and with each other. You notice what's present and what's missing. You ask: what's being rewarded? What do people laugh at? What do they never say aloud?

Slow Values don't have to be imposed – because they already exist. Once uncovered and phrased with care, they feel obvious in the best way. When I sit across the table from an owner or CEO and share my recommendations, I'll often witness a struggle between understanding and confusion in their initial responses – *Isn't that what we've always said?*

The truth is that they have recognised them immediately because they've been living them all along and seeing other people do the same, or because they have recognised their absence in those who just don't seem to fit. Those values have been there without the words. And because the values are true, they're far easier to instil. Not just through posters or campaigns, but through use in decisions, conversations, priorities. That's how they move from tacit to active.

8. Slow Values feel tangible.

A criticism people often level at values is that they are fluffy, and I am generally inclined to agree.

Values too often lean towards the nice. The starting point is the question: 'What can we do, as a business, to make ourselves more palatable to the outside world?' It's the wrong question, which dooms the process from the outset.

Take Enron, the American commodities giant. Its values included the standard junk favourites, 'integrity' and 'respect' among them. When the company collapsed in scandal, with leaders jailed, pensions wiped out, and billions lost for investors, its values were revealed for what they really were – hollow words – adding hypocrisy and naivety to Enron's crimes.

Another reason for these justifiable accusations of fluff is the sheer lack of critical evaluation involved in coming up with these words. Bring together a small group of people and ask them a question they don't fully understand and the end result is junk. It's almost impossible to avoid when you consider the politics of the group, the context of the work, and the hopeful expectation that this group will have the requisite skills to arrive at the right answer in just a few hours.

Slow Values are not fluffy. They are true, appropriate, and tied to actions. This makes people more willing to give them a try, even the cynics, because they understand them and can see what they mean. Before long, they will start to experience the benefits of those actions: the process is about consistency and persistence, allowing the culture you are aiming for to emerge, seemingly organically, over time.

9. Slow Values shape behaviour

Behaviour is the result of our values, whether we have expressed them or not. Without values put into words, people will behave as they see fit or based on what they see around them. That's why it's often your equivalent of the kids at the back of the bus who set the culture in the absence of a formally agreed approach.

But get the right values in place and you will find that, not only do they give you a strong foundation on which to plan activities and make leadership decisions, but also that, for the rest of your team, they will clarify what's appropriate, constructive, and expected. They reward the right actions and challenge the wrong ones, without needing an exhaustive list of dos and don'ts.

10. Slow Values wrap round everything

When I help companies to establish and work with their values, we cut and dice their business, which enables us to focus on small areas, pilot schemes, and tailored activities. My goal is to move us away from departmental responsibility

('HR will take it from here'), seniority precedence ('The guys on the production line will never get it.'), and locational variations ('Let's not worry about Argentina, we never see eye to eye.').

The reason is simple: values cannot be left to one department, one level of seniority or one branch of the organisation.

When values are left to HR, they are seen as an HR initiative, not a business one. This applies just as much to marketing, say, or the senior leadership team – which, after HR, are the most common departments saddled with the task of launching the values into actions.

If values are framed as the preserve of seniority, they risk becoming seen as top-down or capped at a lower limit. And when locations and departments are written off, values fracture, creating parallel cultures that compete rather than cohere.

The alternative is to start small and start everywhere. By piloting values across functions led by a widely representative group we see them tested, challenged, and proved in daily practice. That evidence builds trust. It shows people that values are not just a management initiative, but tools for real decisions.

Values spread by demonstration, not decree. They belong to everyone, everywhere.

My method, 5Ps, focuses on People, Publicity, Processes, and Partnerships to lead us towards exceptional Performance. It's good to start your rollout by bringing together a small cross-section of action-focused people from across the business. They will generate ideas about how each value can be brought to life within each of the four active Ps. And they keep in mind your goal – what does great Performance mean in your business?

This team can form the basis of your culture champions, a group of bright stars who will share responsibility for keeping this commitment to values in action going. (If you wonder who'd join your group, think of the people who have light in their eyes, fire in their bellies and who you'd love to grow, not lose.)

We are looking for lots of small actions, not a few big ones. And crucially, we are looking at stitching these values into the work we do – the work we *need* to do, the work that is fundamental to our business. I have noticed that very often this values work is treated as a project, with its own new actions. But the truth is, whilst reflection will undoubtedly reveal things you could be doing better or for the first time, the sweet spot is when you build your values into core business activities.

From recruitment to feedback, team meetings to decisions, Slow Values are embedded into your rhythms and rituals. This builds consistency and helps them become an intuitive feature of life in your business.

11. Slow Values underpin accountability

What is made public is made real, and what gets measured gets done. Once you have uncovered your values and expressed them well, started to put the actions in place, and selected your culture champions, you'll see greater accountability.

I knew this was working in my business when I accidentally overheard a conversation between two colleagues – great mates – who were critiquing a piece of work one of them had done that the other found lacking. This was not their comfort zone, it's fair to say. In fact, I had never heard them having this kind of tough chat before. But they were able to do so using the values phrases we had in place.

We see personal accountability increase but also a greater sense of peer accountability, which leads to more open conversations, higher standards, and improved performance. This sense of responsibility across levels and departments is not dependent upon hierarchical imposition of rules, but rather underpinned by a sense of shared direction and principles.

12. Slow Values build trust

Trust isn't only about results. It comes from knowing how decisions will be made, and why. Over time, Slow Values create that sense of predictability.

Greggs is a popular high-street bakery, and also one of the UK's most effective businesses. Its values – friendly, inclusive, honest, respectful, hardworking – are present in the business's daily decisions. These might be single words, dangerously close to Junk Values, but they are at least true. Managers are trusted to lead with autonomy. Teams include ex-offenders who have been given a proper second chance. Profits are shared across the business. During the pandemic, Greggs showed responsibility by topping up pay and protecting jobs.

This culture of trust shows in the results: loyal customers, low staff turnover, steady growth, and a £1.5 billion market value.

Slow Values support this. When values are embedded, behaviour becomes consistent. That consistency builds trust. And trust is the platform for long-term performance.

13. Slow Values have power

Sometimes, it feels like everything is a power struggle, doesn't it? From tantrumming toddlers to querulous elderly parents, from generational dynamics in the workplace (good luck, building understanding between your long service Boomers and your new starter Gen Zs, who are both absolutely certain they're right) to protracted negotiations with clients and suppliers.

Now, whilst we can't individually solve the global macroeconomic power shift that's inexorably changing the rules around us, what we can do is place ourselves in a position of responsiveness, not reaction. And this applies whatever the power struggle.

Slow Values bring clarity about what matters and how to behave, so decisions don't always have to be made by the most senior people in the team. This reduces the need for top-down control, making it easier to spread responsibility without things unravelling. Power can be shared more evenly across the business without inviting chaos.

And because everyone understands the rules of the game, teams can act with confidence, consistency, and purpose.

14. Slow Values can contain contradictions

Within any set of Slow Values, there will always be the possibility of contradiction. Take phrases that boil down to the sentiments of honesty and kindness. Clearly, these two things can sometimes pull in different directions.

A leader might find themselves weighing up whether to deliver a hard truth in simple clear terms or whether to soften it in order to preserve someone's dignity. Neither choice is wrong, what matters is recognising the tension and consciously deciding which value best serves the situation.

That is the strength of Slow Values. They are not rigid commandments, but a living framework for judgement. In practice, this means knowing your values well enough to also know which to choose when they seem to clash, and having the confidence to stand by the value that best supports your purpose, your people, and the outcome you seek.

Over time this builds consistency, integrity, and trust because people can see not only what you decided, but why.

15. Slow Values withstand pressure

… more than that. Slow Values earn their spurs when the pressure is on. It's all very well to have a lovely set of touchy feely values saying that everyone matters (BrewDog, anyone?), but if that doesn't apply when cashflow's tight, projects are overrunning, and clients are threatening to pull the plug, then they are not your values at all.

Imagine you are in a situation where neither answer is good. Maybe you have to make the choice between two possible redundancy candidates, maybe you need to decide whether to fire a client, maybe you need to close a factory or end a programme. As a leader there are inevitably times that you have to make choices that don't fill your heart with joy.

And that is why we have values.

Because if you can't make a nice choice, you can still make a right choice.

Our values really aren't our values until we have had to make a decision that hurts in the short term in order to help us deliver on our longer-term goals. Lencioni refers to this as your pain point. Without the right values that's incredibly hard to do.

With Slow Values, it's possible, and the more you do it, the clearer it will become that your Slow Values are an invaluable business asset.

Could you make those choices with Junk Values? Maybe. Would you trust that choice? I doubt it.

When faced with two bad options,
which of your values will guide
the least damaging and most
principled choice?

Who in your business is
confident enough to act on values
without asking permission?

Looking back, which recent decision
would you change if you had used
your values as the deciding test?

Chapter 10

HEN'S TEETH

Hen's teeth are in short supply. So are Slow Values.

Now, whilst hen's teeth are purely metaphorical, Slow Values are entirely possible and yet still vanishingly rare.

You can lament this, or you can use it to your advantage. Because if, amongst your peers, you are the only one who is doing this the slow way, you're going to gain a significant competitive advantage that covers everything from talent acquisition to retention, from efficiency to profitability, from brand awareness to reputation, from market position to trust.

I used to express surprise that more businesses didn't have good quality, genuine values since establishing them is purely common sense. I've learned not to say that. Quite clearly, the scarcity of clear, bespoke values demonstrates that to forge and deploy them is a rare skill indeed.

Hen's teeth is about values that are essentially organic and regional since their provenance is impeccable. They are developed in a considered manner, with patience. The research that leads to them is undertaken with curiosity, active listening, astute thinking, and creative expertise to develop accurate and actionable insights.

These types of values have the advantage of not needing to be launched because they have emerged over time.

A striking example comes from Great Ormond Street Hospital. When they set about developing their values, they asked not just the board or the leadership team, but 2,644 patients, families, and staff. The question was simple: *what difference do we make when we are at our best?*

The answers were shaped into values, which were then broken down into tangible expressions. Take their focus on families. It's expressed in two areas – welcoming and helpful – and then distilled further into four clear sub-points. Each one shows not only the behaviours people want to see, but also the opposite behaviours they don't.

This clarity is what makes them powerful. Don't just say it, explain it. And don't be afraid to use the counter-example. Knowing what something isn't can be just as helpful as knowing what it is. That honesty gives people confidence, and it sets boundaries that everyone can understand.

> GOSH values
>
> **Welcoming**
>
> **People want to see staff who are...**
>
> - Open to everyone regardless of views, culture, ideas, role or seniority
> - Positive and cheerful, with an enthusiastic attitude

- Warm, making people feel welcome
- Polite ('Hello, my name is…, my role is…, and may I…')
- Prompt, valuing others' time and keeping waiting to an absolute minimum
- Thoughtful, making waiting feel less anxious or boring
- Respectful, treating individuals as unique
- Considerate of people's feelings.

Helpful

People want to see staff who…

- Go out of their way to be helpful, even beyond their role
- Are patient, making enough time for people
- Flexible, with a 'can-do' attitude and keeping promises
- Accountable, taking responsibility for their actions
- A role model in all they do.

Expert

People want to see staff who…

- Are calm, putting people at ease
- Consistently practise high standards of safety and hygiene
- Are vigilant – speaking up when safety is compromised
- Constantly strive for quality, always aiming for better outcomes
- Are proactive, using research and learning to improve
- Seek innovative solutions to problems.

One Team

People want to see staff who…

- Are willing to listen and hear people
- Are informative, ensuring people know what's happening
- Are mindful to explain clearly, speaking on a level with people
- Are proactive in involving patients, families, and colleagues
- Are keen to share knowledge, information, and learning
- Are appreciative, offering open, honest feedback
- Act as positive advocates, encouraging others to speak up.

It's not for nothing that the French call the boss 'chef' because leadership is still required whilst gathering these ingredients to make the perfect Slow Values. Sometimes, people think that the work you do to understand people and draw them into the progress is about abdication of leadership. That's not true.

The best values come about by honouring the blend of leaders' decisions and wider insights, involvement, and integration. You cannot effectively communicate with people whose language and motivations you don't know. You may share words with them that their brains understand but you will not capture their hearts.

This takes time, and it is the thing that underpins genuine shared direction and unity, which are often referred to as 'clarity and alignment'.

Let's look at COOK, the frozen meals company that's been providing excellent and seemingly homecooked food to the hungry and pecunious since 1997. It's heavily values driven, and those values display every sign of being homecooked too. The dead giveaway for this is value two: Churchill's Pig.

Does that mean anything to you? Unless you know COOK, I'd guess not. But this is what they tell people it means:

> The pig was Winston Churchill's favourite animal.
>
> He reckoned that a cat looks down on a man, a dog looks up to a man, but a pig looks a man in the eye and sees his equal.
>
> This sums up the way we talk to each other and our customers with absolute honesty and openness, looking each other in the eye as equals. There's no 'them' and 'us'. We own up to our mistakes and we don't do hidden agendas.
>
> We're all pig: no bull.

In other words, respect. That word is one of our top 24 Junk Values, a regular guest in lazily developed, potentially damaging values sets. But COOK has taken the concept and made it their own. I can almost guarantee that you won't find Churchill's Pig in any other set of values. It sits alongside:

> **Be part of our family:** Only by working together as one can we achieve our goals. We all have different roles, different abilities and different personalities: by

collaborating we can do remarkable things. We look out for each other, look after each other and muck in where necessary. Like all families, sometimes we'll fall out but we always make up after a row.

Be remarkable: We all have the potential to do a remarkable job. This means doing our work in such a way that someone else can't help remarking how great it is.

Have fun: We spend more hours working than doing anything else (unless you sleep A LOT). Let's make sure we enjoy it and have fun. We take our work seriously but that shouldn't mean we take ourselves too seriously.

Care: Caring takes effort, not money. It's how we deliver quality in everything we do. If we care about our kitchen, our food, our shops, our service, our customers, our colleagues and our communities, it will make a huge difference. The more we care, the bigger the difference and the more pride and satisfaction we can take in our work.

And these 'Essential Ingredients' come together to ensure: "Combine our Essential Ingredients in just the right way and you get remarkable COOKies."

When I see these values, I see the signs of Slow Values. Even the order is considered – team comes first, when it so often comes last – and the quirky values phrases can be comfortably explained with a few brief sentences. Only one of them, care, is a single word, and a precipitously close to Junk Value word at that, but COOK lives it.

COOK enjoys an exceptional 5-star TrustScore from over 37,000 reviews, with 87% of reviewers awarding five stars and just 2% leaving one-star ratings. Customers consistently praise the food quality and customer service. The company responds to 95% of reviews within 24 hours, applying the respect inherent in the value described as Churchill's Pig.

On Glassdoor, 76% of team members say they would recommend working at COOK. Reviews indicate a positive internal culture, particularly in relation to their values and working environment, with no significant issues reported.

These are values which not only set out behavioural expectations but also underpin the organisational brand. They are a resonant demonstration of Cook's personality and make it very clear what really matters.

COOK's values are not so far away from the norm that they are hard to understand – words like care, family, and fun often crop up – but they are very definitely unique. If you walk into any branch of COOK, visit the website, or even contact the founder on LinkedIn, you will experience these values.

Some other quirky values

Airbnb: 'Be a cereal entrepreneur'

This one of Airbnb's values is designed to keep them nimble. It refers to a wild idea hatched when Airbnb was seriously in debt and bookings were barely trickling in. Their solution? Cereal boxes. Obama-O's, the breakfast of change, and Captain McCain's, a maverick in every bite, were sold for $40 a box during the 2008 party conventions and almost cleared the debts.

It revealed the grit and creativity that Brian Chesky believed should always define Airbnb, no matter how big the business became. To be a cereal entrepreneur is to embody that resourceful conviction that even the daftest idea might just be the one that saves you.

IBM: 'Treasure wild ducks'

This is along similar lines to Chesky's cereal. Thomas J. Watson Jr. was chairman from 1961 until he retired in 1971. That was the period when IBM transformed from a mid-sized business machines company into a global computing giant and when he coined and lived by the reminder to 'keep the wild ducks flying.'

This is a reference to Danish philosopher Kierkegaard's journal observations of how wild geese can become tamed by consistent interaction with tame geese. Kierkegaard concludes 'The law for genius is this : A tame goose never becomes a wild goose but on the other hand a wild goose can certainly become a tame goose – therefore watch out!'

And what benefit does this kind of bespoke values development bring? Isn't it easier to simply grab the values equivalent of a drive-thru or even a fabulous pre-made frozen meal from, for example … COOK?

The truth is that the difference between something ubiquitous and something unique is fundamental to the impact of your values. Here's a baker's dozen of how Slow Values prove their worth as you use them to build your culture.

1. Intuitively lived

When the values you set out are the real values of place, people will refer to them in everyday decisions, not just in board meetings and training sessions. Because they are a reflection of the deep-rooted personality of your business, albeit you at your best, there will be an element of intuitive behaviour that you can build on.

2. Your language

Every tribe has its own dialect. Idioms, nicknames, or mottos arise naturally and stick. The process of listening properly to gather this vocabulary, of understanding and interpreting how it's used, leads to values which are expressed in the language of your people. That means they will use them because they use it.

3. Environmental values

Developing Slow Values requires an understanding of your ecosystem, not just its people. That includes your environment. And then once this is understood, it becomes the basis for further development. So, you are starting a circular process where existing choices define the values, which then underpin new choices that help you to fill existing gaps and build up from the right place.

4. Moral glue

When your values are your values, you will find that team

members and community members willingly act in line with them, often without instruction. In fact, the values become the glue that creates a sense of belonging: of being 'crew' and at the heart of this thing.

When people inevitably face decisions that test their moral mettle, the values will enable them to make decisions that they, their colleagues, and you can trust; if they make the wrong decision, the values allow you, their colleagues, and them to understand why it was wrong.

5. Unscripted use

I walked into a clients' meeting room to prepare for a chat. Another meeting had just finished and I spotted a scrap of paper on the table, on which someone had written WE GO HIGH! in capital letters, with a Sharpie, putting three lines under the word high.

Curious, I asked one of the team what had gone on. There'd been a disagreement. It was nothing dramatic but instead of letting it fester, they'd pulled the conversation back to the values. One of them had even said, 'Let's try and do this the high way,' which I'm told raised a smile.

Get the right values in place and you will see people correct each other (and themselves) when behaviour drifts.

6. Launch is for wimps

Slow Values development brings people in early and grounds the work in real practice and local insight. By the time the values are agreed, they're already partly embedded.

There's no need for a big launch.

Instead, begin drawing them out with your people either as a values team or through another style of group that is representative of the business as a whole, inviting their help to bring them into the heart of the business and apply them. That's as close to a launch as you'll ever need to get.

7. Brand distinction

Slow Values stand out. When you build your values from the inside out with texture, tone, and provenance, your organisation stops sounding like everyone else and starts standing for something unique. It's the difference between own-brand and owning your voice.

8. True you

True values clarify who you are and what you're not. That makes decisions faster, positioning easier and messaging sharper. When a team lives by values that are trusted and nourishing, their actions create a character that customers, partners, and colleagues can recognise and rely on.

9. Customer loyalty

Whilst I have some reservations about Simon Sinek's hugely famous Start With Why proposition, I do agree that differentiation is essential and needs to capture people's imaginations. When values are visible in every interaction, they create emotional allegiance. Customers become advocates. Loyalty deepens not just because of practical marketing mechanics, but because customers see themselves and their own values reflected in yours.

10. Tested reputation

Your reputation is tested in hard times. If your values are real, your response to a crisis will be too. Businesses with Slow Values don't flounder or flip-flop; instead, they respond with consistency and integrity. That builds lasting reputational strength and earns respect, even when things go wrong.

If you need to ask what your position is on a matter of ethics and your values are not giving you the answer, then they're probably junk.

11. Market value

Companies with real values attract investors, partners, and acquirers who are in it for the long term. Not private equity that wants to sweat you, squeeze you, and shut you down. Culture is not about pizza meetings and beanbags; it's about shared goals and responsibility.

Companies with a consistent values-led culture that is delivering great performance are seen as lower risk and higher trust. This type of culture adds tangible value to the balance sheet, and Slow Values are its cornerstone. They signal maturity, responsibility, resilience and potential.

12. Brand resilience

Once values are firmly planted, they don't rely on a communications strategy to be understood. They are visible in what you do. That makes you less vulnerable to leadership changes or market trends because your point of reference is internal, not external.

13. Story writes itself

With Slow Values, your living story emerges naturally. Your team shares anecdotes, your customers build their view of you around this language, and your culture becomes a compelling narrative.

With the right assets in place, you will see this cultural identity unfold every day, in every meeting, by the way you act, by your treatment of customers, your product quality, and everything else besides. This builds understanding and sets expectations on all sides.

Do your values need to be announced, or are they apparent in the everyday life of your business?

Where do your values make your business unmistakable in its choices, stories and behaviour?

How will you prove to customers and partners that your values are more than posters or website copy?

Chapter 11

THE HUMAN ONION

It's your birthday and you're celebrating by taking yourself to a restaurant. It's a treat you've been looking forward to for a little while. So you get dressed up in a swanky outfit, call an Uber, and set off. On arrival, you're greeted by polite, cheerful staff and shown to a table that's in the perfect spot for people-watching.

Water is brought, your napkin shaken out and placed on your lap. After a few minutes, you start to wonder where the menu is. Ten minutes pass and still no menu has arrived, so you ask a waitress.

She looks quite surprised to be asked. 'We don't do menus here', she says, 'we serve what the chef wants to cook and the staff want to bring to you.'

Disconcerted, you settle back and await what's coming. Soon, your plates start to arrive. They're a bit of a hotchpotch of dishes, some healthy and some less so, some traditional and some rather cutting-edge; some are warm and some are cold, some are unexpectedly delicious and some revolt you.

There's a sense of expectation surrounding you as you receive these treats. The chef's looking at you through the glass, the waitress keeps checking your progress, fellow diners are glancing in your direction. You're here, you're hungry, and you don't want to disappoint them, so you give every dish a try.

This meal is representative of beliefs.

Your beliefs are a product of what matters to other people. You don't choose your beliefs; instead, they grow within you based on your experiences. Sometimes, these are things we encounter at home, sometimes, at school, maybe in our early career. In many cases, we will have forgotten the precise incidents that forge our beliefs, but through consistency, they become engrained.

My model, The Human Onion, describes the layers of experience, personality, and choices that make us, us. Tucked deeply down in the onion, you'll find two layers that are intimately connected to one another. Combined, they are the Circles of Choice: individually, they are Beliefs and Values.

When we start to question our beliefs and work towards defining our values, we are moving further from surface-level choices and closer to the core of what makes us our own masters.

The Human Onion

I help people to dig deep.

Because while most of us would like to live from the inside out – guided by purpose, rooted in values, acting with intention – it rarely starts that way. We're shaped by what's happening around us. We react before we reflect.

That's why, in values-led growth, we begin at the edges and work our way inward.

This is the premise of The Human Onion, a model I use to help people and organisations make sense of what powers them. The name is light-hearted, but it reflects the truth that each of us is multi-layered. Remember Shrek and donkey in the onion field? Those layers have a clear order, and self-awareness comes from working through them one by one. We begin with the outer world, then peel back to what's most enduring.

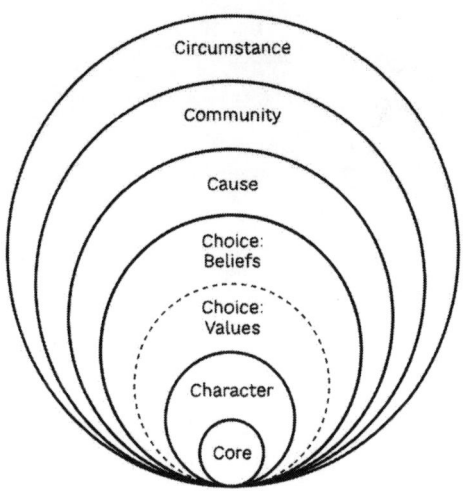

Circumstance

The outer layer is where most of us spend our time. Our lives can pass endlessly juggling demands, dealing with change and trying to keep up. These are your current conditions: job roles, deadlines, domestic responsibilities, financial pressures …

You can't always influence your circumstances. But you can decide whether to react or respond. That decision launches the process of change.

Community

The next layer we inspect features your relationships. These are the people around you at home, at work, in your hometown, your wider network, even people you read about in the news or see on social media. This layer influences you more than you might realise.

Belonging is powerful. But the question is: are you moulding yourself to fit, or are you participating in a way that reflects who you are?

Cause

Now we reach the layer of motivation. Your Cause is your sense of purpose. Crack purpose and you unlock the source of your power.

Some of you will have a clear idea of your purpose and will have whittled it down to a point that is sharp and clearly defined. For others, your understanding of purpose arrives slowly, as you experience more of the joys and tribulations of life. It guides your behaviour and gives you the impetus to want to live in a way of which you can be proud. For Aristotle, a life with purpose was the greatest form of happiness. He called it eudaemonia.

If you lose sight of your Cause, it's hard to feel that your work, your relationships, or your choices really matter.

Choice

This is the layer where change happens, and it's what I spend a great deal of time focusing on with my clients. In between these two lines is the shift you can make from living by unconscious inheritance – beliefs – and moving to live instead by conscious intention – values.

- **Beliefs** tend to be shaped by experience, culture and upbringing. These are often absorbed rather than consciously selected. They can be helpful but often they hold us back.
- **Values** are shaped through thought and understanding. These are the things you choose to live by, once you've done the work to understand what matters to you.

Have you spent time considering whether the things you hold as values are actually beliefs? Once you have identified whether your beliefs are helpful, you are ready to dig deeper into what matters most.

If you can change the dynamic between the layers so that you live by your values and let them guide your beliefs, you have reached a significant turning point.

Character

Here you'll find your most natural self: the tendencies, instincts, and ways of being that come easily to you.

Some of this is temperament. Some you learn early and it settles. This layer becomes easier to understand and work with once your values are in place.

What's natural isn't always helpful, and you might not like everything about yourself in this layer. But when it's well directed or effectively managed, it can be powerful.

Core

At the centre of it all is your Core. You could call it your soul. It doesn't change with the weather. It isn't shaped by other people. It is yours. It may be covered over, quietened, or out of reach for a while, but it's always there. And when you connect with it, everything else starts to make sense.

The Human Onion model is a useful tool to approach your growth in a logical, compassionate way. By beginning at the outer layers and working inwards, you start to uncover what really matters to you. Once you understand this, you can begin to live in a way that feels driven by what's at the centre of the onion rather than being dictated by circumstances or buffeted by the waves of others' opinions.

The aim is not perfection, but what Srikumar Rao calls Mastery: to be self-possessed, to honour what you feel matters most, to let your values shape your leadership, to be proud of yourself.

What is the best way to start this process? As always, start with a question. Think of something that you suspect might be a belief rather than a value and ask yourself, 'Where does that come from?'. If you track it back to a parent, school mate, boss, or old friend, to something you read in a book, heard in a film, or saw in an ad campaign, or something that happened to you, then it's a belief.

It's time for the next question. Does that belief help you or might it hinder you instead? This choice is in your hands. If you realise something you have held dear for a long time is standing in the way of progress, diverting you from your purpose, and impeding your quality of life, you are quite within your rights to change it. You can honour it without adhering to it.

We often have a sentimental attachment to our beliefs. That doesn't mean we need to live by them. I have fond memories of Mum preparing an ox tongue, studded with cloves, and pressed under bricks, every Christmas. I didn't like eating it then and I certainly wouldn't eat it now.

So, if your belief is limiting, you can make the decision to move on from it. But if you find your belief is fundamental to the life you want to live, then consider integrating it into your values. You'll maybe want to shake it up a little bit – put it in your language, not your grandmother's – but celebrate it and build on it. It's looked after you so far, and it'll stand you in good stead for the years to come.

Imagine now that, instead of being served dishes chosen by others, you were handed a menu. It's comprehensive, to say the least. Some items are highly rated by other diners, some recommended by the team, some approved by critics; there are a few images of celebrities eating their own favourite food there too. Other items on the menu are less popular, they're getting negative reviews. There are exciting, new-sounding dishes, restaurant staples, and some classics you'd forgotten.

You have complete freedom to choose the items you want.

Your values are not formed of other people's wishes, nor of what people want you to accept. You are not the mouthpiece for someone else's vision, nor a supporter in their campaign. That a critic rates it, a singer eats it and 200 diners like it has no connection at all to your choices. You choose the dishes that you want, and I can guarantee you'll have a meal that not only fills your belly but warms your cockles too.

Your values do not need to be fashionable, popular, or influencer-led. They need to be the things that mean most to you, allow you to define the course of your own life. Do you remember that scene in *Runaway Bride* where Richard Gere, rematched with goofily gorgeous Julia Roberts, helped her decide what kind of eggs she liked, rather than allowing her to simply choose her potential husband's favourite? That was love: giving her the power of choice rather than imposing his choice on her.

And funnily enough, once you are clear in your own values, you are far more tolerant of other people's.

So, how does this apply to business?

As I look around, I see hosts of companies confusing beliefs with values. Junk Values are a dead giveaway, because if you don't feel something you won't understand it, and if you don't understand it, you can't explain it in your own language.

Einstein is attributed with saying, 'If you can't explain something simply, you don't understand it well enough'. If you are using values that can be found on the list of Junk

Values, you are taking refuge in buzzwords because you haven't dug deep enough.

Maybe you formed your values in a facilitated workshop, which took place in the course of half a day. Maybe you developed them with a small group, a group in which the politics of work roles or prejudices and relationships influenced people's suggestions. Maybe you came up with them yourself but wanted to ensure they got buy-in, so kept them fairly neutral.

There is no neutrality in values. To be unremarkable is to create a vacuum in which you lose control of the narrative. So, these apparently safe choices are actually dangerous.

If you're not sure, have a look at your company's values and ask yourself a few questions.

> Where does this come from?
>
> Is it helping us or holding us back?
>
> Do we actually believe it, or just fear what would happen if we didn't say it?
>
> Can we make good choices with these values?
>
> Are values hiding beneath these beliefs?

Don't let yourself off the hook. These are questions that merit deep thought, taking yourself into some uncomfortable places, coming up with honest answers. A few squeamish moments will help you move towards a much stronger position.

What are real values, really?

They are crafted, tested, and adjusted until they work. They emerge from your unique character as a business and reflect its context. They're about what's right for you, not what's generally considered to be right. They take time. They are trustworthy. They do not reflect fads or fashions. You cannot be pressured into having them by other people or organisations.

And in return for their individuality they guide you, they ensure you can act with integrity, and they pretty quickly form collective moral muscle memory.

By contrast, the beliefs that you think are values keep you in a world of shoulds and musts. Shoulds are not from you but from others, musts are pressurising and unrewarding, and the combination of the two make beliefs burdensome and hard to honour.

Which of your current values are inherited beliefs that no longer serve your business?

If your values disappeared from view tomorrow, could people still describe how to live them?

Where are you letting unchallenged beliefs inform decisions instead of consciously chosen values?

Chapter 11

THE HEAT AND THE HUNGER

Time, I am afraid to say, for a BFRC.

Big Fat Reality Check.

Most people go to work to earn a living. They're not on a lifelong quest for meaning; they're just trying to get through the day, do a decent job, and get home. For them, and often for the managers overseeing them, the subject of values can sound detached from the real pressures of working life. It can feel indulgent, irrelevant, a distraction from the demands of their jobs. This does not make them bad team members, and their cynicism is understandable.

Especially when all they see is stated values that are undeniably jargon. Junk.

Many businesses fall into the trap of believing that their people don't care about the company's purpose, which is why their values never really take hold. It becomes easy to explain away disengagement. If your people are disinterested in your purpose, that must be the problem, not the possibility that the values themselves are off the mark or that the purpose itself is misphrased.

Almost every time I start work with a new client I'll be told that one area of the business is essentially a no-go zone. The drivers will never buy into this. The guys on the production line will rebel. Middle management will come to values meetings but refuse to change their ways.

But they must and they will – the drivers will take it on board, the production team will build it in, management will see transformation and want more – if you do this the right way, not the quick way.

The truth is that people *do* want something to care about. You might call it vision and purpose. It's so much more rewarding to have a job that warms the soul than one that just covers the rent. And as generations change, that need is becoming more prominent. People may cover it up with cynicism, but if you give them a reason to care, something they really have a reason to believe in, you can build a sense of purpose that starts to power something rather exciting.

You need to find the heat, a shared spark that ignites the team, and the hunger, the reason to bother in the first place.

Purpose gives you the appetite to act. Sometimes, purpose is phrased in an emotionally resonant way and sometimes it's purely practical. I like to compare the style of Maya Angelou's words: 'My purpose is life is not merely to survive, but to thrive; and to do so with some passion, some compassion, some humor and some style.' with the classic explanation of the purpose of a hammer: 'to hammer in nails'.

You need to know your people well enough to know which type of purpose will strike a chord. If you have a very mission-focused team they'll warm to something with the poetic and aspirational edge of Angelou's statement. If your team is full of practically minded do-ers, then find your hammer.

Vision is the heat. It energises and gives momentum, creates a sense of onward movement, and must be set out in terms that ignites your people's spark, not just the Board's. The story I share is of Winnie the Pooh, who was so excited by the sight and smell of honey in a nearby tree that despite being a lazy, tubby bear, he tried to get the honey by climbing the tree and floating up towards the tantalising treat using a balloon. He made an effort. He came up with solutions. Not bad for a bear of very little brain.

That's what a good vision does. It makes people want to try.

My question to you is this. What is your people's honey? It's unlikely to be the same figures that excite you: the pounds, percentages, EBITDA, SKUs, etc., etc., etc. Equally, it's not to be found in three paragraphs of management speak.

A great vision is succinct and taps into your people's inspiration. Patagonia's vision is to 'save our home planet'; IKEA's is 'to create a better everyday life for the many people'. The purpose of a vision is to inspire your people: it's that simple. Vision may well not be shared externally, meaning that you can really fine-tune it to what your people care about most.

Because when you serve something real, people will come for it. They're interested, willing to try, they talk about it amongst themselves, they feel energised.

Vision and purpose can fall just as easily into the junk trap as values. But if you do your research, use some creative insights, tap into what motivates people, you can express your vision and purpose in ways that the whole team will care about.

That's where Slow Values come in. Because once people care – once the heat and the hunger have taken hold – they need the right tools to act. And Junk Values won't do the job. They're neither strong enough nor specific enough to guide behaviour or sustain progress. Slow Values, on the other hand, give people a way to progress. They translate belief into action.

That's what Active Ethos® does.

If you apply Active Ethos®, you'll see your values deliver excellence. Build and reward that hunger, turn up the heat and they will come.

Active Ethos® is a practical model for building a strong, high-performing culture by connecting four essential elements: vision, purpose, values, and everyday behaviour.

It starts with a clear **vision**. This is the shared goal that brings people together and gives direction. A good vision is energising. It shows where you're heading and gives people something to work towards. Without it, effort becomes scattered and motivation fades.

Your **purpose** then makes that vision matter. It's the reason your organisation exists; the useful, clear, and true explanation of the difference you make. If vision is the destination, purpose is why it's worth getting there. When people understand both, they begin to care, and when people care, they commit.

That commitment needs to be supported by strong values. These aren't generic statements, buzzwords, or easy. They're the principles that define how your organisation works at its best. Values guide decisions, shape expectations, and set the tone for how people work together.

When you support the build of values to the point where they are lived by everyone, every day, they shape your **culture**. They help to overcome generational differences and create a connection. They appear in how you solve problems, how you treat people, and how you uphold standards inside the business and out in the world. That's 'you' as a team, not as a lone voice for values.

A strong, consistent culture earns trust. And trust supports so many good things. It gives you the freedom to make choices, to experiment, even to fail once in a while.

You'll see it in your results – not just financial, but also in the quality of your relationships, the strength of your reputation, and your ability to stay resilient in the face of change and challenge.

Are your vision and purpose
clear enough to fuel values
or are they word soup?

Which story best demonstrates
your values in action, and how
often are you retelling it?

Where does pressure risk burning
out your values and what's your
discipline to keep them intact?

Chapter 12

USE YOUR ENERGY

You're hungry. It's hours since breakfast and you're in a rush to get to the next meeting. It's a crucial conversation with a potential investor and you need your wits about you. You want to build your energy levels quickly so you pop into a fast food outlet and grab a value meal. As suddenly as it arrives, the tray slid across the counter with a shout of your order number, it's in your belly. You've quite possibly eaten it whilst walking.

You arrive at the meeting, grimly conscious of your greasy hands and the clinging odour of chip fat. But at least you've primed your energy levels. You feel as alert as a squirrel, focused and on form.

The meeting starts, as they do in Britain, with pleasantries about travel, the weather, and pending or recent school holidays/weekends. Tea is offered and accepted, a plate of chocolate-coated biscuits put into the middle of the table. Everyone settles into their seats, coughs, papers are picked up, and Remarkables primed for notes. Someone's phone rings, they fumble to turn it off, a domino ripple of phone-checking finally dies down, and the meeting can start.

Meanwhile, your body's been at work. It's gone into crisis mode, releasing a medicinal dose of insulin to counteract the sugars, salts, and chemicals you've just poured down your throat. Suddenly, you feel drained and lethargic, like you can't quite lift your arms from the meeting table. Your focus blurs and the guy chewing his gum to your right triggers intense irritation. The sound of it slapping round his tongue, as he masticates it with his mouth half open, distracts you from the conversation round the table as you self-protectively zone out.

Hang on. What's that?

Silence … an embarrassed silence. All heads have swivelled in your direction and the meeting's Chair is saying your name, clearly not for the first time: it has an almost visible question mark attached.

You've fallen at the first hurdle, and now you're struggling to remember what you'd planned to say.

Junk food gives us a hit of energy, which wears off pretty quickly as our bodies go into defensive mode, fighting to process the stuff that gives us that salty, fatty satisfaction. We don't just lose the energy we've gained, but crash as tiredness and irritation consume us, with physical impacts including shaking, nausea, and brain fog.

This is a metaphor for what happens when we use the wrong kind of fuel in life, and in business. And just like food, values are only useful if we can absorb and act on them.

Otherwise, they're dead weight.

Imagine instead you'd made yourself lunch that morning whilst the kettle boiled for your morning mug of tea. You'd packed the lunch in your rucksack and taken the opportunity to find a park bench before you arrived at the meeting. Stopping to eat allows you to clear your mind of what came before, and prepare it for the meeting ahead of you. You can review your notes, double-check your intentions, and take a few deep, slow breaths.

You arrive at the meeting nourished in body, mind and spirit. The food you prepared releases energy slowly for a few hours, comfortably taking you to the end of the session and beyond with consistent levels of personal energy and a good sense of focus.

Because you chose well, you have been well set up for success. The benefits of your choice passed, in many ways, unnoticed. Steady energy is invisible but essential to support our daily lives whether you're dealing with tricky meetings or taking your kids to soft play over the weekend.

Let's now imagine, however, that you'd eaten that healthy lunch, but instead of going to a meeting afterwards, you'd stayed on the park bench all afternoon.

The energy your food created would be stored, tucked away in your liver, muscles, and fat cells. If you did that every day, before long you would start to put on weight and lose muscle density; after some time, you could possibly even develop a disease.

However good our food is, we need to convert its energy to good use. It's the combination of good fuel and good action that makes us healthy. And the same is true of your business.

If you took every step in this book towards developing a great set of Slow Values but then stuck them up on the wall and forgot about them, you'd be doing yourself damage. If you don't say what your values are, people will guess from what they see. If you're decent, functional people then the guess will probably be quite flattering. But if you state your values and go to the trouble of making them easy to read, then any behaviour at odds with those words will cause cynicism, discord, and loss of trust.

Values are energy, and energy is meant to be used. Values power everything, if you use them well. For that to happen, you need to metabolise them. Because they will only fuel your business when they're digested fully into decisions, behaviours, and expectations.

You need to build the organisational equivalent of a healthy gut, where values are recognised, absorbed, and turned into action. That's when they become strength: they'll even generate their own energy.

Values aren't an initiative. They're an operating system. And like any good system, they need to be embedded everywhere so they deliver the performance you're aiming for.

The 5Ps

The 5Ps model is the combination of actions across People, Publicity, Processes and Partnerships to define Performance. I developed this method to chop through the usual silos we see in companies – departments, locations, levels of seniority – and instead focus on seeding values through people everywhere, in everything they do, all the time.

I'm a great believer in lots of small actions, rather than one or two big initiatives. If you're wrapping your values around things that already happen in the business, they become an integral part of its daily rhythm, not a standalone project. Some will flourish, others may fade; but the risk of failure is mitigated by the sheer range of activities.

And to be clear, these are all fundamental to your business's purpose, not extras. We are talking here about core ingredients, not garnish.

You bring people alongside you. In all but the most micro of microbusinesses, this is not for one person to deliver. A values team or culture champions will help to plant and nurture this in areas you don't even see and, in doing so, shine a light on those areas for you too.

Who are your culture champions? They're your stars. Not your SLT, or your HR team, or your marketing department, but people at all levels from every part of the business. Choose your brightest sparks and make it their opportunity to show you what they're capable of, given the opportunity and your trust. You are quite probably putting at least some of your succession plan in place at the same time.

At the heart of the model is **Performance**. Be clear about what great performance means to you. Ideally, sum it up in a single word. It might be loyalty, reach, trust, profit, efficiency, or something unique to your sector. That clarity gives direction. What do you want to achieve?

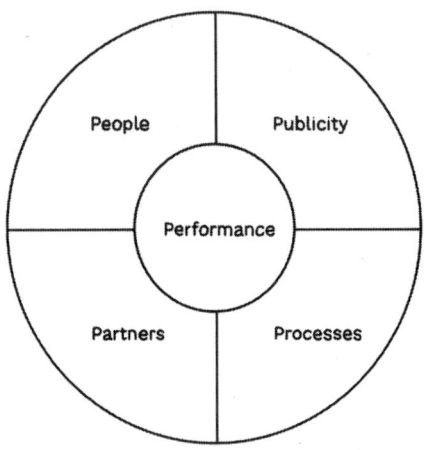

These four areas – People, Publicity, Processes, and Partners – shape and support your Performance.

- **People** includes everyone who works with or for you, regardless of contract. It covers recruitment, induction, development, and how people leave.
- **Publicity** includes every internal and external communication, from packaging and press to internal campaigns and community engagement.
- **Processes** covers everything from strategic direction to everyday interactions, including (especially!) the ones furthest from your sight.

- **Partners** invites you to select and manage your suppliers, clients, and collaborators with the same thoughtfulness you bring to your own team.

The 5Ps model helps you to design and harness your culture, rather than letting values sit in a document gathering dust, apparent only in a few posters dotted about the office and an annual awards ceremony. With 5Ps, they become working tools and an invaluable ongoing asset.

When you consider People, your aim is to embed values into everyday thinking, language, and behaviour. That means sharing stories, being entirely clear about what each value means in context, and encouraging feedback opportunities that make values feel real and not just rhetorical. Recruitment, development, mentoring and performance all become opportunities to explore and strengthen the sense of shared values. Done well, this gives people a deep sense of purpose and belonging.

Publicity, which is often the first place where values appear visibly, must go far beyond posters and slogans. This is about showing, not telling. Values should be evident in how you present your organisation to the world, from tone of voice to colour palette, from campaigns to charity and community work. Internally, too, values shape announcements, recognition, and day-to-day conversation.

What tools can you use to really help people understand what these mean, why they're important, how they're working? This is your opportunity to create cultural 'Ah ha!' moments.

How do you explain your values to people? As well as extensive contextual descriptions, for example, in job descriptions, it's useful to have a short, sharp, multi-application explainer.

Here's how Wikimedia does it. I have shown their value, 'We are in this mission together', as an example.

> **We are in this mission together.**
>
> We believe this because …
>
> - We solve problems better through collaboration.
> - We find joy, belonging, and connection in doing things together.
> - We have to balance individual priorities with our shared collective responsibilities.
>
> In practice, this means …
>
> - I support my colleagues whenever I can, and ask for help whenever I need it.
> - I help figure out the problem when I disagree with a proposal.
> - I work towards real decisions, a shared agenda, and clear accountability.

And here's how my agency, Spring, did it:

> **1. Bring Positive Energy.**
>
> - **Means that:** We approach everything with energy and positivity.
> - **My perspective:** 'I am full of enthusiasm right now!'
> - **My effect on others:** 'I am gathered up by the momentum and confident about this person's ability. I feel excited.'
> - **In one word:** Enthusiastic

2. Know What Matters.

- **Means that:** We find out what's important, and focus on it.
- **My perspective:** 'I've really got my head round what's needed here'
- **My effect on others:** 'I am sure this person understands what we need to do. I feel safe.'
- **In one word:** Focused

3. Make Excellent Work.

- **Means that:** We devise, maintain, and deliver the best response to briefs.
- **My perspective:** 'I'm as good as my best piece of work. This is going to be it.'
- **My effect on others:** 'From first to last, this person's work has been dependably good. I feel thrilled.'
- **In one word:** Uncompromising

4. Improve People's Lives.

- **Means that:** We make things better for our clients, their customers, our community, and ourselves.
- **My perspective:** 'I'm in this for the positive impact it has on my fellow human beings.'
- **My effect on others:** 'This person has focused on what I need, as well as my customers. I feel good.'
- **In one word:** Empathetic

5. Live our Vision as Agents for Change.
- **Means that:** Everything we do supports change: we know the change and make it happen.
- **My perspective:** 'I can change the world, right here!'
- **My effect on others:** 'I knew things needed to change, and this person helped me do it. I feel proud!'
- **In one word:** Ambitious

Processes are the systems that keep culture consistent. This is where values become the standard against which decisions are made and behaviours assessed. Whether you're starting a meeting, solving a problem, or signing off a new strategy, the question is: how are our values supporting this?

This goes right through from your business plan – not just its content but even its format – to your project management planning and delivery, to how your frontline staff are representing your culture.

Of the four Ps, Partners is the one most often overlooked and therefore presents a great opportunity for values growth. These are the people and businesses beyond your payroll, but still central to your impact. Ever been let down by a supplier and had to take responsibility for it with the client? Ever sacked a client because they're sending your team's morale through the floor and, if you don't, good people will leave?

This is exactly why clients and suppliers must be chosen with the same care and clarity you bring to building your team.

If you're serious about your values, they need to be built into your supply chain, procurement, external communications, and collaborations. When partners share your values, it improves relationships from the off, supports honest conversations, and helps to ensure successful outcomes.

Think about the partners you have now. Did you choose them carefully? Are expectations clear? Is there formal agreement about values and behaviour? What impact does value clashes have on everyone's work?

You've gone to the trouble of creating those wonderful values. Ignore them, and you might stagnate. Use them, and you will flourish.

Where in your recruitment, development, and performance systems are values made explicit and measurable?

Which of your processes ensures people choose by values rather than by convenience?

Do your suppliers and partners understand and echo your values and, if not, why are you still working with them?

CONCLUSION

IN CONCLUSION

I wrote this book to challenge the standard lazy approach to values, an approach that is as ubiquitous as multinational fast food outlets in town centres and out-of-town shopping destinations, as damaging as two-litre bottles of fizzy pop and oversized 'sharing' bags of crisps, and as unhealthily normalised as tackling obesity with an injection or gut health with a branded drink.

In building my own practice, I have refused to tread the well-worn path of half-day workshops producing a list of five clichéd values words. My clients would be wasting their time and money and I would be dishonouring my profession. Even if the time taken and the money spent is lower, it is wasted; in fact, it's an investment in decline.

Long ago, I made my peace with the realisation that most companies and people I work with will not come to me until all the pans are bubbling over, fat's spitting, and the kitchen's filled with smoke. Because culture is like the air around us: we don't even notice until it gets poisonous.

Most businesses will happily stick with what they have. Most people will not consider their values. They will be absolutely fine until those pans catch fire and they're absolutely not.

But if you are of the mind to work on your values the slow way, to put in the time and effort and thus reap the inevitable rewards, I hope this book has enlightened and inspired you to plant the seeds, grow the veg, make the soup, and flourish.

Here are three things to chew on:

- If you've skipped the groundwork, go back. There are no shortcuts to culture.
- If your values aren't quite ringing true, question and challenge them. Make them real.
- If you've done the work, keep it alive. Slow Values need consistent application to nourish you and your business.

Looking back to the start of this book, where I broke my life into sections related to its connection between food and values, where am I now?

After we sold our agency, I took the leap (some called me brave ... always an unnerving description to have levelled at you!) and focused my attention wholly on this subject.

Career-wise, I went from a strategic, creative, growth-creating generalist to a strategic, creative, growth-creating specialist. I moved from a respected position in an established market to becoming a disrupter in a sector that's infused with bad practice and lazy answers.

The big difference is that now I have access to the very deepest places in companies' DNA and the very deepest reaches of people's lives. It's a phenomenal privilege to be trusted with such honesty, rawness, and need: one I honour fully.

I've seen the impact of limiting beliefs, of not having the values to hand to protect you from other people's contradictory purpose, of corporate terrorists who've found the gaps in culture and stretched them to breaking point.

I've seen what happens when values emerge in their true form, the power it gives to people, teams, and brands.

I've stepped back and admired the moment clients begin to bring this into the heart of things for themselves, making it fully theirs.

All of this means I have learned to observe the world in a new way. I've seen the reasons that despotic leaders behave as they do and the weaknesses in the system that allow them to take hold; the reason why highly funded lobbying groups can seize and own the narrative with such damaging consequences. And I've witnessed what happens when people and organisations who have fallen prey to these things find their feet, their heart, their soul, and their voice and re-emerge to make better choices.

In my own life, I have moved from the product of my ancestral family tree to the product of my choices, keeping what works for me and moving away from those beliefs that don't. I have gained a life that meets my scrutiny, without 'shoulds' or 'musts'.

I take joy from my fabulously international blended family with whom I eat laksa and lasagne, Sunday Roast and sushi. I revel in the company of my colourfully uncoordinated friends, not a group so much as a handpicked selection of the best, brightest, and most soul-stirring people, with whom I share deep conversation, wilful encouragement, and plenty of Yorkshire Tea. In choosing only clients whose cause really fires me up, I meet challenge and stimulus with every new project and destination: not to mention gaining friends for life whilst also experiencing a smorgasbord of corporate catering.

I am still determinedly climbing the mountain, fuelled by passion and determination, set on my intention to plant the flag for the brilliance of Slow Values when I get to the summit. I have faith in my views and feel curious about those which might seem to conflict with them. I defend what must be defended and move on from that which does not. You might not like some of my opinions and I might not like some of yours, but there is more that unites us than divides us and that's what I take joy in unearthing.

I wish you well for your own Slow Values: values that nourish you, values that last. You can follow me on LinkedIn for regular updates, and find out more at erikaclegg.com. And who knows, maybe we'll meet one day.

When we do, I'd love to hear your story, too.

What is your 90-day plan
to embed Slow Values into
decisions, culture, and growth?

When the next crisis comes, what
kind of decision will prove your
values are real and who will be
accountable for making it?

Who will you work with to make
sure your values aren't junk, and
what's stopping you from starting
that conversation today?

APPENDICES

Appendix A:

THE TOP 100 MOST OVERUSED VALUES WORDS

These are the words that keep coming up, time and time again. The words with asterisks are the top 24. I'm not saying don't use them: I am saying include them in your thinking. But then dip deeper and aim higher. Remember Churchill's Pig? That's respect, but memorable and characterful.

1. Ethics
1. Accountability*
2. Duty
3. Fairness
4. Honesty*
5. Integrity*
6. Reliability
7. Respect*
8. Responsibility*
9. Transparency
10. Trust*

2. Relationships
11. Collaboration*
12. Communication*
13. Community*
14. Compassion
15. Diversity*
16. Empathy
17. Inclusion*
18. Kindness
19. Service*
20. Teamwork*

3. Performance
21. Achievement
22. Ambition
23. Commitment*
24. Excellence*
25. Ownership*
26. Performance*
27. Professionalism
28. Quality*
29. Results
30. Success

4. Responsibility
31. Care
32. Citizenship
33. Environment*
34. Ethics
35. Safety
36. Security
37. Stewardship
38. Sustainability*
39. Responsibility (social)*
40. Wellbeing

5. Determination
41. Boldness
42. Courage*
43. Determination
44. Drive
45. Leadership*
46. Passion*
47. Perseverance
48. Persistence
49. Resilience
50. Strength

6. Innovation
51. Adaptability
52. Agility
53. Change
54. Creativity
55. Curiosity*
56. Growth
57. Learning
58. Imagination
59. Improvement
60. Innovation*

7. Optimism
61. Energy
62. Enthusiasm
63. Fun
64. Happiness
65. Hope
66. Inspiration
67. Joy
68. Motivation
69. Optimism
70. Positivity

8. Harmony
71. Balance
72. Calm
73. Flexibility
74. Harmony
75. Health
76. Order
77. Peace
78. Stability
79. Tranquillity
80. Work–life

9. Efficiency
81. Accuracy
82. Consistency
83. Dependability
84. Discipline
85. Effectiveness
86. Efficiency
87. Focus
88. Organisation
89. Precision
90. Punctuality

10. Ambition
91. Aspiration
92. Future
93. Growth mindset
94. Opportunity
95. Potential
96. Progress*
97. Purpose*
98. Success
99. Vision
100. World-class

Appendix B

JUNK VALUES FIELD SPOTTER'S GUIDE

Like horse's teeth, Junk Values are easy to spot once you know what you're looking for. Use this guide as your notebook for sightings in the wild whether on a works bus, a website, a poster behind reception, or a recruitment ad. The more you notice them, the sharper your eye will become.

SIGHTING NO. 1

Date: ....

Place: ....

The values:

....

....

....

....

....

Why they are junk:

☐ *Sound like everyone else's*

☐ *Too vague to guide behaviour*

☐ *Hard to remember*

☐ *Zeitgeisty buzzword*

☐ *Other*

Clues that confirmed my suspicion:

....

....

....

SIGHTING NO. 2

Date: ....

Place: ....

The values:

....

....

....

....

....

Why they are junk:

- ☐ *Sound like everyone else's*
- ☐ *Too vague to guide behaviour*
- ☐ *Hard to remember*
- ☐ *Zeitgeisty buzzword*
- ☐ *Other*

Clues that confirmed my suspicion:

....

....

....

SIGHTING NO. 3

Date: ....

Place: ....

The values:

....

....

....

....

....

Why they are junk:

☐ *Sound like everyone else's*

☐ *Too vague to guide behaviour*

☐ *Hard to remember*

☐ *Zeitgeisty buzzword*

☐ *Other*

Clues that confirmed my suspicion:

....

....

....

SIGHTING NO. 4

Date: ....

Place: ....

The values:

....

....

....

....

....

Why they are junk:

☐ *Sound like everyone else's*

☐ *Too vague to guide behaviour*

☐ *Hard to remember*

☐ *Zeitgeisty buzzword*

☐ *Other*

Clues that confirmed my suspicion:

....

....

....

SIGHTING NO. 5

Date: ....

Place: ....

The values:

....

....

....

....

....

Why they are junk:

☐ *Sound like everyone else's*

☐ *Too vague to guide behaviour*

☐ *Hard to remember*

☐ *Zeitgeisty buzzword*

☐ *Other*

Clues that confirmed my suspicion:

....

....

....

SIGHTING NO. 6

Date: ....

Place: ....

The values:

....

....

....

....

....

Why they are junk:

☐ *Sound like everyone else's*

☐ *Too vague to guide behaviour*

☐ *Hard to remember*

☐ *Zeitgeisty buzzword*

☐ *Other*

Clues that confirmed my suspicion:

....

....

....

SIGHTING NO. 7

Date: ....

Place: ....

The values:

....

....

....

....

....

Why they are junk:

☐ *Sound like everyone else's*

☐ *Too vague to guide behaviour*

☐ *Hard to remember*

☐ *Zeitgeisty buzzword*

☐ *Other*

Clues that confirmed my suspicion:

....

....

....

Appendix C:

GLOSSARY OF TERMS

When it comes to values, culture and all that surrounds them, you'll encounter different interpretations of the same words. Hopefully what those words mean to me is evident by the context in which they appear, but in case they need clarification, here's my glossary of terms.

I'd strongly recommend that you actually avoid using most of these words when you work on your values, since they can be rather divisive. Consider how Pepsi, Amazon, GOSH and others have ripped up not just the words for their own values but also for the whole ecosystem to ensure it feels relevant.

Purpose

Your reason for being. Why you are here, why you bother, what sits at the heart of your organisation. Simon Sinek calls it your 'why'.

Mission

Your unique purpose, the reason you exist that sets you apart from your peers. Your mission statement sets this out in clear and accessible terms.

> *A note on purpose and mission:* Mission is planned and active, whereas purpose is more intuitive and internal. For example, my own purpose is *to prosper, and to cause others to prosper*, whereas my mission is to instil Active Ethos® wherever teams are a stranger to high-performing culture.

Vision

The guiding ambition for your organisation. When well-phrased, it gives everyone something to get behind and makes it worth their while to live your values. Essential for leadership.

Credo

One essential, overriding belief, which in its way is as important as your vision. Mine is that everything good should flourish.

Mantra

A phrase that encourages and sustains your team when resilience is needed or the going gets tough. This might be your why, your credo, or something based on personal outcomes and rewards. Mantras can be circumstantial.

Beliefs

The things you, or you and your team, hold to be true, whether right or wrong. Sometimes helpful, sometimes limiting.

Values

The things that are important to you, your principles and standards. It is vital to set values that you feel in your belly or you will find them hard to stick to.

> Patrick Lencioni divides values into four types; you might find this useful when you explore yours:
>
> - Core values: Deeply ingrained, never compromised, distinctive.
> - Aspirational values: Desirable but not yet real, not to be confused with core values.
> - Permission-to-play values: Baseline standards, like honesty, which don't differentiate.
> - Accidental values: Emerge unconsciously from team interests or demographics; can help or hinder. These are what I tend to refer to as beliefs.

Ethics

Your principles and moral choices, closely related to values.

Ethos

A driving force that defines your approach, attitude, and ambitions – the spirit of place. It is perceived from actions and implications, shaping how others experience your organisation.

Behaviours

The way your values come to life to form culture. Behaviours are how your culture is carried into the world. You will need planned, tracked, and managed activities to inform those behaviours, especially at the start of the process when nothing is intuitive and the benefits are not yet visible.

Actions

The real-world, day-to-day deliverables by your team that express your culture in practice.

Active Ethos®

The process of defining and phrasing your ethos, then bringing it to life fully and sustainably in every aspect of your organisation. It is about capturing the spirit of place and embedding it through values-driven behaviours to deliver culture. I call it Active Ethos® rather than Active Values because it is more than a list of principles; it is their relentless application to create a high-performing culture.

Culture

The behavioural environment you create that carries your values through your people. This is the big ticket item, and the 'active' part of Active Ethos® is designed to address it. If you do not manage it, other factors will. Hence the famous quote, 'Culture is what happens when you're not in the room.'

Brand

The intuitive and expressed articulation of your culture. It is how people perceive you and the expectations they hold about your approach, quality, service, and product.

THANKS AND PRAISE

It takes a village to raise a child, and a team to launch a book. My thanks to the people who have helped me get Junk Values out of my head and onto your shelf.

> Wise counsel: Simon Hazelgrove
>
> Design: Bex Spillings
>
> Cover illustration: EVIL CREATIVES
>
> Diagrams: Tom Baines
>
> Author photograph: Jonathan Sapsford
>
> Appendix illustrations: Blue
>
> Proofreading: Ariane Laurent-Smith
>
> Publicity: Deborah Watson
>
> Social media management: Miri Birch
>
> Tea and peace: The Swan Hotel, Southwold

ABOUT ERIKA

Born in Hertfordshire and raised in Lancashire, Erika Clegg DL FRSA has lived happily on the Suffolk Coast for many years having spent her twenties in London. Much of the time she can be found in trains, planes or her bright yellow car, bouncing between assignments.

She and her husband founded the brand communications agency, Spring, shortly after their wedding in 2005. They grew it into a national and international player - albeit one based in the seaside market town of Southwold - before its senior leadership team took the reins in 2022. During that time Erika also sat on the board of the Design Business Association, the national voice for design effectiveness, and on various regional arts boards.

Fuelled, motivated and occasionally exasperated by values, she has devoted her recent career to helping people and organisations distinguish between the junk and the good stuff. She helps them to pinpoint their purpose, direction and principles with absolute clarity and relishes seeing the benefits unfold as this turns into action and results.

Beyond work she is a wife, mum and stepmum, with a lively household that includes dogs, cats and a constant flow of family and friends.

A keen Peloton rider, she thrives on challenges and is always up to something new - from planning her first novel to tackling long-distance walks for charity. Erika is honoured to serve as a Deputy Lieutenant of Suffolk, with a focus on supporting the RNLI, championing the arts and strengthening community life.